TEACHER'S PET PUBLICATIONS

LITPLAN TEACHER PACK
for
Othello
based on the play by
William Shakespeare

Written by
Mary B. Collins

© 1996 Teacher's Pet Publications
All Rights Reserved

This **LitPlan** for William Shakespeare's
Othello
has been brought to you by Teacher's Pet Publications, Inc.

Copyright Teacher's Pet Publications 1996
11504 Hammock Point
Berlin MD 21811

Only the student materials in this unit plan (such as worksheets,
study questions, and tests) may be reproduced multiple times
for use in the purchaser's classroom.

For any additional copyright questions,
contact Teacher's Pet Publications.

www.tpet.com

TABLE OF CONTENTS - *Othello*

Introduction	11
Unit Objectives	13
Reading Assignment Sheet	14
Unit Outline	15
Study Questions (Short Answer)	19
Quiz/Study Questions (Multiple Choice)	25
Pre-reading Vocabulary Worksheets	35
Lesson One (Introductory Lesson)	49
Nonfiction Assignment Sheet	52
Oral Reading Evaluation Form	56
Writing Assignment 1	58
Writing Assignment 2	64
Writing Assignment 3	78
Writing Evaluation Form	65
Vocabulary Review Activities	63
Extra Writing Assignments/Discussion ?s	68
Unit Review Activities	80
Unit Tests	83
Unit Resource Materials	117
Vocabulary Resource Materials	131

ABOUT THE AUTHOR
WILLIAM SHAKESPEARE

SHAKESPEARE, William (1564-1616). For more than 350 years, William Shakespeare has been the world's most popular playwright. On the stage, in the movies, and on television his plays are watched by vast audiences. People read his plays again and again for pleasure. Students reading his plays for the first time are delighted by what they find.

Shakespeare's continued popularity is due to many things. His plays are filled with action, his characters are believable, and his language is thrilling to hear or read. Underlying all this is Shakespeare's deep humanity. He was a profound student of people and he understood them. He had a great tolerance, sympathy, and love for all people, good or evil.

While watching a Shakespearean tragedy, the audience is moved and shaken. After the show the spectators are calm, washed clean of pity and terror. They are saddened but at peace, repeating the old saying, "There, but for the grace of God, go I."

A Shakespearean comedy is full of fun. The characters are lively; the dialogue is witty. In the end young lovers are wed; old babblers are silenced; wise men are content. The comedies are joyous and romantic.

Boyhood in Stratford

William Shakespeare was born in Stratford-upon-Avon, England, in 1564. This was the sixth year of the reign of Queen Elizabeth I. He was christened on April 26 of that year. The day of his birth is unknown. It has long been celebrated on April 23, the feast of St. George.

He was the third child and oldest son of John and Mary Arden Shakespeare. Two sisters, Joan and Margaret, died before he was born. The other children were Gilbert, a second Joan, Anne, Richard, and Edmund. Only the second Joan outlived William.

Shakespeare's father was a tanner and glovemaker. He was an alderman of Stratford for years. He also served a term as high bailiff, or mayor. Toward the end of his life John Shakespeare lost most of his money. When he died in 1601, he left William only a little real estate. Not much is known about Mary Shakespeare, except that she came from a wealthier family than her husband.

Stratford-upon-Avon is in Warwickshire, called the heart of England. In Shakespeare's day it was well farmed and heavily wooded. The town itself was prosperous and progressive.

The town was proud of its grammar school. Young Shakespeare went to it, although when or for how long is not known. He may have been a pupil there between his 7th and 13th years. His studies must have been mainly in Latin. The schooling was good. All four schoolmasters at the school during Shakespeare's boyhood were graduates of Oxford University.

Nothing definite is known about his boyhood. From the content of his plays, he must have learned early about the woods and fields, about birds, insects, and small animals, about trades and outdoor sports, and about the country people he later portrayed with such good humor. Then and later he picked up an amazing stock of facts about hunting, hawking, fishing, dances, music, and other arts and sports. Among other subjects, he also learned about alchemy, astrology, folklore, medicine, and law. As good writers do, he collected information both from books and
from daily observation of the world around him.

Marriage and Life in London
In 1582, when he was 18, he married Anne Hathaway. She was from Shottery, a village a mile from Stratford. Anne was seven or eight years older than Shakespeare. From this difference in their ages, a story arose that they were unhappy together. Their first daughter, Susanna, was
born in 1583. In 1585 a twin boy and girl, Hamnet and Judith, were born.

What Shakespeare did between 1583 and 1592 is not known. Various stories are told. He may have taught school, worked in a lawyer's office, served on a rich man's estate, or traveled with a company of actors. One famous story says that about 1584 he and some friends were caught poaching on the estate of Sir Thomas Lucy of Carlecote, near Warwick, and were forced to leave town. A less likely story is that he was in London in 1588. There he was supposed to have held horses for theater patrons and later to have worked in the theaters as a callboy.

By 1592, however, Shakespeare was definitely in London and was already recognized as an actor and playwright. He was then 28 years old. In that year he was referred to in another man's book for the first time. Robert Greene, a playwright, accused him of borrowing from the plays of
others.

Between 1592 and 1594, plague kept the London theaters closed most of the time. During these years Shakespeare wrote his earliest sonnets and two long narrative poems, 'Venus and Adonis' and 'The Rape of Lucrece'. Both were printed by Richard Field, a boyhood friend from Stratford. They were well received and helped establish him as a poet.

Shakespeare Prospers
Until 1598 Shakespeare's theater work was confined to a district northeast of London. This was outside the walls, in the parish of Shoreditch. Located there were two playhouses, the Theatre and the Curtain. Both were managed by James Burbage, whose son Richard Burbage was Shakespeare's friend and the greatest tragic actor of his day.

Up to 1596 Shakespeare lived near these theaters in Bishopsgate, where the North Road entered the city. Sometime between 1596 and 1599, he moved across the Thames River to a district called Bankside. There, two theaters, the Rose and the Swan, had been built by Philip
Henslowe. He was James Burbage's chief competitor in London as a theater manager.

The Burbages also moved to this district in 1598 and built the famous Globe Theatre. Its sign showed Atlas supporting the world-hence the theater's name. Shakespeare was associated with the Globe Theatre for the rest of his active life. He owned shares in it, which brought him much money.

Meanwhile, in 1597, Shakespeare had bought New Place, the largest house in Stratford. During the next three years he bought other property in Stratford and in London. The year before, his father, probably at Shakespeare's suggestion, applied for and was granted a coat of arms. It bore the motto Non sanz droict-Not without right. From this time on, Shakespeare could write "Gentleman" after his name. This meant much to him, for in his day actors were classed legally with criminals and vagrants.

Shakespeare's name first appeared on the title pages of his printed plays in 1598. In the same year Francis Meres, in 'Palladis Tamia: Wit's Treasury', praised him as a poet and dramatist. Meres's comments on 12 of Shakespeare's plays showed that Shakespeare's genius was recognized in his own time.

Honored As Actor and Playwright

Queen Elizabeth I died in 1603. King James I followed her to the throne. Shakespeare's theatrical company was taken under the king's patronage and called the King's Company. Shakespeare and the other actors were made officers of the royal household. The theatrical company was the most successful of its time. Before it was the King's Company, it had been known as the Earl of Derby's and the Lord Chamberlain's. In 1608 the company acquired the Blackfriars Theatre. This was a smaller and more aristocratic theater than the Globe. Thereafter the company alternated between the two playhouses.

Plays by Shakespeare were performed at both theaters, at the royal court, and in the castles of the nobles. After 1603 Shakespeare probably acted little, although he was still a good actor. His favorite roles seem to have been old Adam in 'As You Like It' and the Ghost in 'Hamlet'.

In 1607, when he was 43, he may have suffered a serious physical breakdown. In the same year his older daughter Susanna married John Hall, a doctor. The next year Shakespeare's first grandchild, Elizabeth, was born. Also in 1607 his brother Edmund, who had been an actor in London, died at the age of 27.

The Mermaid Tavern Group

About this time Shakespeare became one of the group of now-famous writers who gathered at the Mermaid Tavern in Cheapside. The club was formed by Sir Walter Raleigh. Ben Jonson was its leading spirit (see Jonson). Shakespeare was a popular member. He was admired for his talent and loved for his kindliness. Thomas Fuller, writing about 50 years later, gave an amusing account of the conversational duels between Shakespeare and Jonson:

"Many were the wit-combats betwixt him and Ben Jonson; which two I behold like a Spanish great galleon and an English man-of-war; Master Jonson (like the former) was built far higher in learning;

solid, but slow, in his performances. Shakespeare, with the English man-of-war, lesser in bulk, but lighter in sailing, could turn with all tides, tack about, and take advantage of all winds, by the quickness of his wit and invention."

Jonson sometimes criticized Shakespeare harshly. Nevertheless he later wrote a eulogy of Shakespeare that is remarkable for its feeling and acuteness. In it he said:

> Leave thee alone, for the comparison
> Of all that insolent Greece or haughty Rome
> Sent forth, or since did from their ashes come.
> Triumph, my Britain, thou hast one to show
> To whom all scenes of Europe homage owe.
> He was not of an age, but for all time!
> . . . .
> Sweet Swan of Avon! what a sight it were
> To see thee in our waters yet appear,
> And make those flights upon the banks of Thames,
> That so did take Eliza, and our James!

Death and Burial at Stratford

Shakespeare retired from his theater work in 1610 and returned to Stratford. His friends from London visited him. In 1613 the Globe Theatre burned. He lost much money in it, but he was still wealthy. He shared in the building of the new Globe. A few months before the fire he bought as an investment a house in the fashionable Blackfriars district of London.

On April 23, 1616, Shakespeare died at the age of 52. This date is according to the Old Style, or Julian, calendar of his time. The New Style, or Gregorian, calendar date is May 3, 1616. He was buried in the chancel of the Church of the Holy Trinity in Stratford.

A stone slab-a reproduction of the original one, which it replaced in 1830-marks his grave. It bears an inscription, perhaps written by himself.

On the north wall of the chancel is his monument. It consists of a portrait bust enclosed in a stone frame. Below it is an inscription in Latin and English. This bust and the engraving by Martin Droeshout, prefixed to the First Folio edition of his plays (1623), are the only pictures of Shakespeare which can be accepted as showing his true likeness.

John Aubrey, an English antiquarian, wrote about Shakespeare 65 years after the poet's death. He evidently used information furnished by the son of one of Shakespeare's fellow actors. Aubrey described him as "a handsome, well-shaped man, very good company, and of a ready and pleasant smooth wit."

Shakespeare's will, still in existence, bequeathed most of his property to Susanna and her daughter. He left small mementoes to friends. He mentioned his wife only once, leaving her his "second best bed" with its furnishings.

Much has been written about this odd bequest. There is little reason to think it was a slight. Indeed, it may have been a special mark of affection. The "second best bed" was probably the one they used. The best bed was reserved for guests. At any rate, his wife was entitled by law to one third of her husband's goods and real estate and to the use of their home for life. She died in 1623.

The will contains three signatures of Shakespeare. These, with three others, are the only known specimens of his handwriting in existence. Several experts also regard some lines in the manuscript of 'Sir Thomas More' as Shakespeare's own handwriting. He spelled his name in
various ways. His father's papers show about 16 spellings. Shakspere, Shaxpere, and Shakespeare are the most common.

Did Shakespeare Really Write the Plays?
The outward events of Shakespeare's life are ordinary. He was hard-working, sober, and middle-class in his ways. He steadily gathered wealth and took good care of his family. Many people have found it impossible to believe that such a man could have written the plays. They feel that he could not have known such heights and depths of passion. They believe that the people around Shakespeare expressed little realization of his greatness. Some say that a man of his little schooling could not have learned about the professions, the aristocratic sports of hawking and hunting, the speech and manners of the upper classes.

Since the 1800's there has been a steady effort to prove that Shakespeare did not write the plays or that others did. For a long time the leading candidate was Sir Francis Bacon. Books on the Shakespeare-Bacon argument would fill a library (see Bacon, Francis). After Bacon became less popular, the Earl of Oxford and then other men were suggested as the authors. Nearly every famous Elizabethan was named. The most recent has been Christopher Marlowe. Some people even claim that "Shakespeare" is an assumed name for a whole group of poets and playwrights.

However, some men around Shakespeare-for example, Meres in 1598 and Jonson in 1623-did recognize his worth as a man and as a writer. To argue that an obscure Stratford boy could not have become the Shakespeare of literature is to ignore the mystery of genius. His knowledge
is of the kind that could not be learned in school. It is the kind that only a genius could learn, by applying a keen intelligence to everyday life. Some great writers have had even less schooling than Shakespeare.

Few scholars take seriously these attempts to deprive Shakespeare of credit. Shakespeare's style is individual and cannot be imitated. Any good student recognizes it. It can be found nowhere else. Bacon is a poor candidate for the honor. Great as he was, he was certainly not a poet.

How the Plays Came Down to Us
Since the 1700's scholars have worked over the text of Shakespeare's plays. They have had to do so because the plays were badly printed, and no original manuscripts of them survive.

In Shakespeare's day plays were not usually printed under the author's supervision. When a playwright sold a play to his company, he lost all rights to it. He could not sell it again to a publisher without the company's consent. When the play was no longer in demand on the stage, the company itself might sell the manuscript. Plays were eagerly read by the Elizabethan public. This was even more true during the plague years, when the theaters were closed. It was also true during times of business depression. Sometimes plays were taken down in shorthand and sold. At other times, a dismissed actor would write down the play from memory and sell it.

About half of Shakespeare's plays were printed during his lifetime in small, cheap pamphlets called quartos. Most of these were made from fairly accurate manuscripts. A few were in garbled form.

In 1623, seven years after Shakespeare's death, his collected plays were published in a large, expensive volume called the First Folio. It contains all his plays except two of which he wrote only part-'Pericles' and 'Two Noble Kinsmen'. It also has the first engraved portrait of Shakespeare.

This edition was authorized by Shakespeare's acting group, the King's Company. Some of the plays in it were printed from the accurate quartos and some from manuscripts in the theater. It is certain that many of these manuscripts were in Shakespeare's own handwriting. Others were copies. Still others, like the 'Othello' manuscript, had been revised by another dramatist.

Shakespearean scholars have been determining what Shakespeare actually wrote. They have done so by studying the language, stagecraft, handwriting, and printing of the period and by carefully examining and comparing the different editions. They have modernized spelling and punctuation, supplied stage directions, explained difficult passages, and made the plays easier for the modern reader to understand.

Another hard task has been to find out when the plays were written. About half of them have no definite date of composition. The plays themselves have been searched for clues. Other books have been examined. Scholars have tried to match events in Shakespeare's life with the subject matter of his plays.

These scholars have used detective methods. They have worked with clues, deduction, shrewd reasoning, and external and internal evidence. External evidence consists of actual references in other books. Internal evidence is made up of verse tests and a study of the poet's imagery and figures of speech, which changed from year to year.

The verse tests follow the idea that a poet becomes more skillful with practice. Scholars long ago noticed that in his early plays Shakespeare used little prose, much rhyme, and certain types of rhythmical and metrical regularity. As he grew older he used more prose, less rhyme, and greater freedom and variety in rhythm and meter. From these facts, scholars have figured out the dates of those plays that had none.

Shakespeare As a Dramatist

The facts about Shakespeare are interesting in themselves, but they have little to do with his place in literature. Shakespeare wrote his plays to give pleasure. It is possible to spoil that pleasure by giving too much attention to his life, his times, and the problem of figuring out what he actually wrote. He can be enjoyed in book form, in the theater, or on television without our knowing any of these things.

Some difficulties stand in the way of this enjoyment. Shakespeare wrote more than 350 years ago. The language he used is naturally somewhat different from the language of today. Besides, he wrote in verse. Verse permits a free use of words that may not be understood by some readers. His plays are often fanciful. This may not appeal to matter-of-fact people who are used to modern realism. For all these reasons, readers may find him difficult. The worst handicap to enjoyment is the notion that Shakespeare is a "classic," a writer to be approached with awe.

The way to escape this last difficulty is to remember that Shakespeare wrote his plays for everyday people and that many in the audience were uneducated. They looked upon him as a funny, exciting, and lovable entertainer, not as a great poet. People today should read him as the people in his day listened to him. The excitement and enjoyment of the plays will banish most of the difficulties.

--- Courtesy of Compton's Learning Company

INTRODUCTION

This unit has been designed to develop students' reading, writing, thinking, and language skills through exercises and activities related to *Othello* by William Shakespeare. It includes twenty-four lessons, supported by extra resource materials.

The **introductory lesson** introduces students to Shakespeare and his times through a group research project. Following the introductory activity, students are given a transition to explain how the activity relates to the play they are about to read. Following the transition, students are given the materials they will be using during the unit. At the end of the lesson, students begin the pre-reading work for the first reading assignment.

The **reading assignments** are approximately thirty pages each; some are a little shorter while others are a little longer. Students have approximately 15 minutes of pre-reading work to do prior to each reading assignment. This pre-reading work involves reviewing the study questions for the assignment and doing some vocabulary work for some challenging vocabulary words they will encounter in their reading.

The **study guide questions** are fact-based questions; students can find the answers to these questions right in the text. These questions come in two formats: short answer or multiple choice. The best use of these materials is probably to use the short answer version of the questions as study guides for students (since answers will be more complete), and to use the multiple choice version for occasional quizzes. If your school has the appropriate equipment, it might be a good idea to make transparencies of your answer keys for the overhead projector.

The **vocabulary work** is intended to enrich students' vocabularies as well as to aid in the students' understanding of the play. Prior to each reading assignment, students will complete a two-part worksheet for approximately 10 vocabulary words in the upcoming reading assignment. Part I focuses on students' use of general knowledge and contextual clues by giving the sentence in which the word appears in the text. Students are then to write down what they think the words mean based on the words' usage. Part II nails down the definitions of the words by giving students dictionary definitions of the words and having students match the words to the correct definitions based on the words' contextual usage. Students should then have an understanding of the words when they meet them in the text.

After each reading assignment, students will go back and formulate answers for the study guide questions. Discussion of these questions serves as a **review** of the most important events and ideas presented in the reading assignments.

After students complete reading the work, there is a **vocabulary review** lesson which pulls together all of the fragmented vocabulary lists for the reading assignments and gives students a review of all of the words they have studied.

Following the vocabulary review, a lesson is devoted to the **extra discussion questions/writing assignments**. These questions focus on interpretation, critical analysis and personal response, employing a variety of thinking skills and adding to the students' understanding of the play.

There are three **writing assignments** in this unit, each with the purpose of informing, persuading, or having students express personal opinions. The first assignment is to inform: students take the information they have gathered through research, group work and class discussion and organize it into a composition. The second assignment is to persuade: students attempt to persuade Othello not to kill Desdemona. The third assignment is to give students the opportunity to be creative and express their own opinions: students tell who is responsible for Desdemona's death.

In addition, there is a **nonfiction reading assignment**. Students are required to read a piece of nonfiction related in some way to *Othello*. After reading their nonfiction pieces, students will fill out a worksheet on which they answer questions regarding facts, interpretation, criticism, and personal opinions. During one class period, students make **oral presentations** about the nonfiction pieces they have read. This not only exposes all students to a wealth of information, it also gives students the opportunity to practice **public speaking**. This nonfiction assignment is done in conjunction with the introductory research assignment.

The **review lesson** pulls together all of the aspects of the unit. The teacher is given four or five choices of activities or games to use which all serve the same basic function of reviewing all of the information presented in the unit.

The **unit test** comes in two formats: all multiple choice-matching-true/false or with a mixture of matching, short answer, multiple choice, and composition. As a convenience, two different tests for each format have been included. There is also an advanced short answer version of the unit test.

There are additional **support materials** included with this unit. The **extra activities packet** includes suggestions for an in-class library, crossword and word search puzzles related to the play, and extra vocabulary worksheets. There is a list of **bulletin board ideas** which gives the teacher suggestions for bulletin boards to go along with this unit. In addition, there is a list of **extra class activities** the teacher could choose from to enhance the unit or as a substitution for an exercise the teacher might feel is inappropriate for his/her class. **Answer keys** are located directly after the **reproducible student materials** throughout the unit. The student materials may be reproduced for use in the teacher's classroom without infringement of copyrights. No other portion of this unit may be reproduced without the written consent of Teacher's Pet Publications, Inc.

UNIT OBJECTIVES - *Othello*

1. Through reading Shakespeare's *Othello* students will see how one man's deceitful revenge results in four deaths in the tragedy.

2. Students will demonstrate their understanding of the text on four levels: factual, interpretive, critical and personal.

3. Students will analyze characters to better understand motivation for action.

4. Students will study the theme of revenge and the conflicts of man versus man and man versus himself.

5. Students will learn that prejudice, jealousy and revenge are a part of any historical era, not just modern times.

6. Students will be exposed to background information about Shakespeare, Elizabethan drama, and *Othello*.

7. Students will examine Shakespeare's use of language.

8. Students will be given the opportunity to practice reading aloud and silently to improve their skills in each area.

9. Students will answer questions to demonstrate their knowledge and understanding of the main events and characters in *Othello* as they relate to the author's theme development.

10. Students will enrich their vocabularies and improve their understanding of the play through the vocabulary lessons prepared for use in conjunction with the play.

11. The writing assignments in this unit are geared to several purposes:
    a. To have students demonstrate their abilities to inform, to persuade, or to express their own personal ideas
    b. To check the students' reading comprehension
    c. To make students think about the ideas presented by the play
    d. To encourage logical thinking
    e. To provide an opportunity to practice good grammar and improve students' use of the English language.

12. Students will read aloud, report, and participate in large and small group discussions to improve their public speaking and personal interaction skills.

READING ASSIGNMENT SHEET - *Othello*

Date Assigned	Reading Assignment Act	Completion Date
	I	
	II	
	III	
	IV	
	V	

UNIT OUTLINE - *Othello*

1 Library	2 Nonfiction Reports	3 Materials Parts PV Act I	4 Read Act I	5 Read Act I
6 Study ?s Act I Parts Act II PV Act II	7 Read Act II	8 Writing Assignment 1	9 Study ?s Act II Parts Act III PV Act III	10 Read Act III
11 Read Act III	12 Study ?s Act III Parts Act IV PV Act IV	13 Read Act IV	14 Study ?s Act IV Parts Act V PV Act V	15 Read Act V
16 Study ?s Act V Vocabulary	17 Writing Assignment 2	18 Project	19 Project	20 Extra Questions
21 Writing Assignment 3	22 Film	23 Review	24 Test	

Key: P = Preview Study Questions   V = Vocabulary Work   R = Read

STUDY GUIDE QUESTIONS

SHORT ANSWER STUDY GUIDE QUESTIONS - *Othello*

Act One
1. What was Iago's complaint in Scene I?
2. Who was Brabantio, and why did Iago and Roderigo awaken him in the middle of the night?
3. Why did Iago leave Roderigo at Brabantio's house?
4. What was Brabantio's reaction to Othello's marriage to Desdemona?
5. Why did the Duke send for Othello?
6. Brabantio complains to the Duke about Othello's marriage to Desdemona. After listening to both sides of the story, what was the Duke's reply?
7. What was Roderigo's complaint, and what was Iago's reply to it?

Act II
1. Why did Iago want Roderigo to anger Cassio?
2. What was the purpose of Iago's plan?
3. Why did Iago want Cassio to drink more wine?
4. What lie did Iago tell Montano about Cassio?
5. Why did Othello strip Cassio of his rank?
6. Why did Iago want Cassio to ask Desdemona for help in restoring Othello's faith in Cassio?

Act III
1. Why didn't Iago simply tell Othello right away that Desdemona and Cassio were having an affair?
2. What thing did Emilia find and give to Iago? What did Iago intend to do with it?
3. What was Iago's reply when Othello demanded proof of his wife's disloyalty?
4. What did Othello decide and command at the end of Scene III?
5. What was Emilia's relationship with Iago? Desdemona?
6. Who had the handkerchief at the end of Act III? Why?

Act IV
1. After Iago lied and told Othello that Cassio confessed going to bed with Desdemona, what advice did he give the overwhelmed Othello?
2. How did Iago trick Othello into thinking Cassio was gloating and bragging about his affair with Desdemona?
3. Why was Bianca angry with Cassio?
4. How did Bianca's return with the handkerchief help Iago?
5. Why did Othello hit Desdemona?
6. What was Lodovico's reaction to Othello's behavior towards Desdemona? How did Iago later explain Othello's behavior to Lodovico?
7. Why did Othello ask Emilia about Cassio's affair with Desdemona, and what was her reply?
8. To whom does Desdemona turn for help after Othello calls her a strumpet?
9. Why did Iago tell Rodriego to kill Cassio? Why did Roderigo consent to think about it?

Othello Short Answer Study Questions Page 2

Act V
1. How would Iago gain from Roderigo's death? Cassio's?
2. What happened when Cassio and Roderigo fought?
3. What did Iago do after he wounded Cassio?
4. How was Desdemona faithful to Othello to the end?
5. What was Emilia's reaction when Othello told her that Iago had revealed Desdemona's affair with Cassio to him?
6. Who told the truth about Iago?
7. What happened to Othello, Iago and Cassio in the end?

ANSWER KEY: SHORT ANSWER STUDY GUIDE QUESTIONS - *Othello*

Act One

1. What was Iago's complaint in Scene I?
    Iago has been passed over for a promotion. Cassio got the promotion to Lieutenant even though Iago had more time in service as a soldier. Cassio got the promotion over Iago because his learning included theory and strategy whereas Iago's did not.

2. Who was Brabantio, and why did Iago and Roderigo awaken him in the middle of the night?
    Brabantio was Desdemona's father. Iago and Roderigo awaken him to tell him of Desdemona's marriage to Othello.

3. What was Brabantio's reaction to Othello's marriage to Desdemona?
    He was outraged at this mixed-marriage.

4. Why did the Duke send for Othello?
    "Valiant Othello, we must straight employ you/Against the general enemy in Ottoman."

5. Brabantio complains to the Duke about Othello's marriage to Desdemona. After listening to both sides of the story, what was the Duke's reply?
    The Duke says he thinks Othello would win his daughter as well under the same circumstances, that Brabantio will just have to make the best of the situation.

6. What was Roderigo's complaint, and what was Iago's reply to it?
    Roderigo was love-sick and depressed, seeing no hope for his winning Desdemona now that she is married to Othello. Iago tells him to use his reason, to hold back his passion, that they should "be conjunctive in [their] revenge against him [Othello]."

Act II

1. Why did Iago want Roderigo to anger Cassio?
    Iago told Roderigo that if he can show Cassio as being undisciplined, he can cause "these Cyprus to mutiny" and have Cassio relieved of his duty. This will allow Roderigo a better chance of getting Desdemona, since Othello and Desdemona will have to stay longer until a replacement for Cassio can be found.

2. What was the purpose of Iago's plan?
    By encouraging and using Roderigo, Iago will "put the Moor/At least into a jealousy so strong that judgement cannot cure." Iago will ruin Othello's relationship with Desdemona as a means of revenge for Othello's promoting Cassio instead of himself (Iago).

3. Why did Iago want Cassio to drink more wine?
> He wanted Cassio to be a little drunk and argumentative when Roderigo would approach him later.

4. What lie did Iago tell Montano about Cassio?
> He told Montano that Cassio was drunk every night. He also casted doubt on Othello's judgement for appointing Cassio, who might be drunk in a moment of crisis.

5. Why did Othello strip Cassio of his rank?
> Through Iago's crafty explanation of Cassio's fight with Roderigo, Othello thought Cassio was irresponsible and dishonorable.

6. Why did Iago want Cassio to ask Desdemona for help in restoring Othello's faith in Cassio?
> If Desdemona would take up Cassio's cause, it would appear as though she would favor him. That would advance Iago's plot to make Othello jealous beyond reason.

Act III
1. Why didn't Iago simply tell Othello right away that Desdemona and Cassio were having an affair?
> By being reluctant to tell Othello his thoughts and making Othello drag the information out of him, Iago did lend credibility to his tale and did hold Othello's friendship.

2. What thing did Emilia find and give to Iago? What did Iago intend to do with it?
> She gave him the handkerchief Desdemona had dropped, Othello's first gift to Desdemona. Iago wanted to plant it in Cassio's possession to show Othello that Desdemona had given it as a favor to Cassio.

3. What was Iago's reply when Othello demanded proof of his wife's disloyalty?
> He lied, telling Othello that Cassio had a dream in which he cried out to Desdemona, saying "Let us be wary, let us hide our loves" and "Cursed fated that gave thee to the Moor!" Then Iago told Othello that he saw Cassio with Desdemona's handkerchief.

4. What did Othello decide and command at the end of Scene III?
> Iago was to have Cassio killed within three days. Othello would kill Desdemona himself. Iago was promoted to Lieutenant.

5. What was Emilia's relationship with Iago? Desdemona?
> Emilia was Iago's wife. She did things out of love for him. Emilia was a servant to Desdemona but also had affection and friendship for her. In Act III, Emilia was still more loyal to Iago than to Desdemona; she did not tell Desdemona about the handkerchief.

6. Who had the handkerchief at the end of Act III? Why?
> Cassio gave it to Bianca, his prostitute friend, for her to take out the design.

Act IV

1. After Iago lied and told Othello that Cassio confessed going to bed with Desdemona, what advice did he give the overwhelmed Othello?

    Iago told Othello to forget about it -- that many women end up in beds where they don't belong. He also told Othello to have patience, not to act rashly, to think and protect his own reputation.

2. How did Iago trick Othello into thinking Cassio was gloating and bragging about his affair with Desdemona?

    Iago told Othello that he would question Cassio about his affair with Desdemona. When Cassio comes, Othello retires out of sight, to watch. Instead of questioning Cassio about Desdemona, he asks about his relationship with Bianca, which brought the desired appearances to make Othello's jealousy grow.

3. Why was Bianca angry with Cassio?

    She loved him and thought some other woman had given him the handkerchief as a gift.

4. How did Bianca's return with the handkerchief help Iago?

    Her returning the handkerchief to Cassio made things appear to Othello as though all Iago had said was true; that Desdemona had given the handkerchief to Cassio, who had thought no more of it than to give it to a prostitute.

5. Why did Othello hit Desdemona?

    She, in his eyes, had openly stated her love for Cassio. He was enraged by even the thought of Cassio.

6. What was Lodovico's reaction to Othello's behavior towards Desdemona? How did Iago later explain Othello's behavior to Lodovico?

    Lodovico was shocked, saying that Othello's behavior would not be believed in Venice, and he asked if Othello had lost his wits. Iago replied that this behavior is mild, but he, Iago, can't honestly speak of Othello's behavior, that Lodovico should just observe Othello for himself.

7. Why did Othello ask Emilia about Cassio's affair with Desdemona, and what was her reply?

    He was still looking for truth and proof. Emilia claimed that Desdemona was innocent.

8. To whom does Desdemona turn for help after Othello calls her a strumpet?

    She, ironically, turns to Iago.

9. Why did Iago tell Roderigo to kill Cassio? Why did Roderigo consent to think about it?
   Having Cassio removed at this point removes some possibilities for complications to Iago's plan. Also, having Cassio killed would be sweet revenge for Iago. Roderigo agreed to consider Iago's proposal because Iago had shown him how the removal of Cassio was necessary in the plan for Roderigo's having Desdemona.

Act V

1. How would Iago gain from Roderigo's death? Cassio's?
   If Roderigo would die, Iago wouldn't have to own up to stealing the jewels he was supposed to be giving to Desdemona from Roderigo. If Cassio would die, Iago's lies to Othello would be safe.

2. What happened when Cassio and Roderigo fought?
   Roderigo was wounded by Cassio. Cassio was wounded from behind by Iago.

3. What did Iago do after he wounded Cassio?
   Iago left but returned a few minutes later to "help" Cassio and to finish off Roderigo, who had been identified as one of the attackers.

4. How was Desdemona faithful to Othello to the end?
   When Emilia asked "who hath done this deed" to Desdemona, she replied "Nobody, I myself." She did not tell that Othello had smothered her.

5. What was Emilia's reaction when Othello told her that Iago had revealed Desdemona's affair with Cassio to him?
   She was shocked and amazed. All along she had thought the tale had been a lie contrived by some awful person; never dreaming that Iago was responsible.

6. Who told the truth about Iago?
   Before her death, Emilia told all she had figured out. Then, Iago's actions confessed his guilt. Finally, letters found in Roderigo's pockets made Iago's conviction even more certain.

7. What happened to Othello, Iago and Cassio in the end?
   Othello killed himself. Iago was stabbed and imprisoned, his fate to be determined by Cassio. Cassio became "Lord Governor."

MULTIPLE CHOICE STUDY GUIDE/QUIZ QUESTIONS - *Othello*

Act 1

1. What was Iago's complaint in Scene 1?
    A. Another officer of the same rank was receiving higher pay.
    B. Roderigo cheated during a card game and won.
    C. Cassio got the promotion that he wanted.
    D. He doesn't like the new uniforms that Othello has chosen. He thinks they make the soldiers look like weak women.

2. Why did Iago and Roderigo awaken Brabantio in the middle of the night?
    A. His wife was seriously ill.
    B. A marriage was taking place that involved his family.
    C. Thieves had destroyed his fields and orchards.
    D. There was a plot to murder him that night as he slept.

3. What was Brabantio's reaction to Othello's marriage to Desdemona?
    A. He was joyful and wished them well.
    B. He remained impartial.
    C. He was outraged.
    D. He was not please personally but thought it was good politically.

4. Why did the Duke send for Othello?
    A. The Duke wanted to know which soldiers to promote.
    B. The Duke wanted to send Othello to Ottoman to fight.
    C. The Duke wanted to give Othello a medal for heroism from his last campaign.
    D. The Duke wanted to congratulate him on his marriage.

5. Brabantio complains to the Duke about Othello's marriage to Desdemona. After listening to both sides of the story, what was the Duke's reply?
    A. He agrees to annul the marriage.
    B. He remains impartial, saying a man's personal life is his own business.
    C. He reprimands Brabantio for being a petty gossip and troublemaker.
    D. He says he thinks Othello would win his daughter under the same circumstances, and tells Brabantio to make the best of the situation.

6. What was Iago's reply to Roderigo's complaint?
    A. He told Roderigo to straighten up and act like a soldier.
    B. He told Roderigo to forgive and forget.
    C. He told Roderigo they would work together for revenge.
    D. He told Roderigo to pray to the gods for guidance, then to do whatever they suggested.

Othello - Multiple Choice Study/Quiz Questions Page 2

Act II

1. Why did Iago want Roderigo to anger Cassio?
    A. He thought this would show that Cassio was undisciplined and then he would be relieved of his duty.
    B. He wanted Roderigo to be relieved of his duties.
    C. He thought a fight between Roderigo and Cassio would be a good distraction.
    D. He thought Desdemona would be jealous.

2. What was the purpose of Iago's plan?
    A. to ruin the relationship between Desdemona and Cassio
    B. to make Desdemona jealous
    C. to ruin Othello's relationship with Desdemona
    D. to make Roderigo jealous

3. How did Iago cause Cassio to be argumentative?
    A. Iago discussed politics with him, and purposely disagreed about everything.
    B. Iago made insinuating remarks about Cassio's marital status.
    C. Iago encouraged Cassio to get drunk.
    D. Iago teased Cassio about his weight and age.

4. What lie did Iago tell Montano about Cassio?
    A. He said Cassio had two illegitimate children.
    B. He said Cassio was stealing money from Othello.
    C. He said Cassio had lied about this qualifications to get the position he currently held.
    D. He said Cassio was drunk every night, and would probably be drunk in a moment of crisis.

5. What was the result of Iago's crafty explanation of Cassio's fight with Roderigo?
    A. Othello stripped Cassio of his rank.
    B. They were both put in jail for a month.
    C. Roderigo was banished from the city for a month.
    D. Othello branded them all as troublemakers and refused to listen to them.

6. Why did Iago want Cassio to ask Desdemona for help in restoring Othello's faith in Cassio?
    A. He feels remorse for what he has done.
    B. If she would take up Cassio's cause, it would appear as though she would favor him. That would advance Iago's plot to make Othello jealous beyond reason.
    C. Iago has been secretly plotting with the Ottoman to overthrow the present government. He thinks that if he can weaken the ranks by having them worry about personal problems, the Ottomans will have a better chance of winning the war.
    D. Brabantio has offered to pay him a large sum of money to break up the marriage.

Othello - Multiple Choice Study/Quiz Questions Page 3

Act III

1. Why didn't Iago simply tell Othello right away that Desdemona and Cassio were having an affair?
    A. He didn't think it was important.
    B. He was distracted and forgot.
    C. Not telling added credibility to his story.
    D. He wanted to avoid hurting Othellos with the news as long as possible.

2. What thing did Emilia find and give to Iago?
    A. She found Desdemona's handkerchief.
    B. She found a love letter supposedly written to Desdemona by Cassio.
    C. She found a gold bracelet.
    D. She found Cassio's sword.

3. When Othello demanded proof of his wife's disloyalty, what was Iago's reply?
    A. "Let us hide and ourselves behold the cursed fate of star-crossed lovers."
    B. "Cursed Cassio doth at the midnight hour hold the fair blossom near his heart."
    C. He told Othello he had seen Casio with Desdemona's handkerchief.
    D. He told Othello he had seen Cassio sneak into Desdemona's room.

4. What did Othello decide and command at the end of Scene III?
    A. Iago was to have Cassio killed within three days. Othello would kill Desdemona himself. Iago was promoted to Lieutenant.
    B. Othello would kill Cassio, then hold Desdemona's father hostage to force her to be faithful.
    C. Othello would banish Cassio. Then Iago would pretend to be sympathetic to Desdemona. While she confessed her feelings to him, Othello would be concealed close-by. He would find them, and accuse Desdemona of being unfaithful, and imprison her.
    D. Iago would kill Cassio and Desdemona, making it look like a lover's quarrel.

5. What was Emilia's relationship with Iago?
    A. She was his maiden sister.
    B. She was his daughter.
    C. She was his wife.
    D. She was a slave he had won in battle years ago.

6. Who had the handkerchief at the end of Act III? Why?
    A. Emilia had it, and was planning to return it to Desdemona.
    B. Iago had it to give to Othello.
    C. Cassio gave it to Bianca, his prostitute friend, for her to take out the design.
    D. Desdemona had it; she had found it and didn't tell anyone.

Othello - Multiple Choice Study/Quiz Questions Page 4

Act IV

1. After Iago lied and told Othello that Cassio had gone to bed with Desdemona, what advice did he give Othello?
    A. Othello should have them both arrested.
    B. Ohtello should forget about it and have patience.
    C. Othello should have Cassio arrested.
    D. Othello should confront Cassio and Desdemona.

2. Othello observes Iago and Cassio talking. Who does he think Cassio is talking about?
    A. Desdemona
    B. Bianca
    C. Emilia
    D. Roderigo

3. Why was Bianca angry with Cassio?
    A. He had refused to pay for her services.
    B. She loved him and thought some other woman had given him the handkerchief.
    C. She thought he had been making fun of her to his friends.
    D. He told her he was not going to see her anymore.

4. What was the effect of Bianca's returning with the handkerchief?
    A. Bianca showed her true love for Cassio.
    B. Othello believed Iago's story even more.
    C. Cassio knew then that Desdemona truly loved him.
    D. Iago's plans ere destroyed.

5. Why did Othello hit Desdomona?
    A. She had lied to him.
    B. She had tried to poison him.
    C. She had openly stated her love for Cassio.
    D. She slapped him in the face.

6. What was Lodovico's reaction to Othello's behavior towards Desdemona?
    A. He was shocked.
    B. He applauded.
    C. He laughed.
    D. He stormed out of the room in anger.

7. Who else did Othello ask about Cassio's affair with Desdomona?
    A. Bianca
    B. Emilia
    C. Roderigo
    D. Lodovico

Othello - Multiple Choice Study/Quiz Questions Page 5

8. To whom does Desdemona turn for help after Othello calls her a strumpet?
    A. Cassio
    B. Emilia
    C. Iago
    D. Lodovico

9. Who did Iago tell Roderigo to kill?
    A. Othello
    B. Desdemona
    C. Emilia
    D. Cassio

Othello - Multiple Choice Study/Quiz Questions Page 6

Act V

1. How would Iago gain from Roderigo's death?
    A. His lies to Othello would never be challenged.
    B. His relationship with Desdemona would never be revealed.
    C. He would never have to admit to stealing the jewels.
    D. Roderigo would never tell Cassio about his plot.

2. What happened when Cassio and Roderigo fought?
    A. Roderigo was wounded by Cassio. Cassio was wounded from behind by Iago.
    B. They killed each other.
    C. Iago wounded Roderigo and accidentally killed Cassio.
    D. Cassio wounded Roderigo. Roderigo wounded Cassio.

3. What did Iago do after the battle?
    A. He left but returned a few minutes later to "help" Cassio finish off Roderigo.
    B. He ran away and told Othello what had happened.
    C. He immediately sent for the guards and positioned himself so that he would not be suspected in the fight.
    D. He laughed and loudly proclaimed victory for himself.

4. How was Desdemona faithful to Othello to the end?
    A. She held on to his handkerchief and professed her love for him.
    B. She offered to go to confession, do penance, and anything else Othello asked of her.
    C. She cried and said she forgave him.
    D. She did not tell Emilia that Othello was the one who had smothered her.

5. What was Emilia's reaction when Othello told her that Iago had revealed Desdemona's affair with Cassio?
    A. She said she had suspected it all along. She was glad it had finally come out in the open.
    B. She covered her ears and refused to listen.
    C. She was shocked and amazed. All along she thought the tale had been a lie contrived by some awful person; never dreaming that Iago was responsible.
    D. Although she publicly supported her husband, she was furious with him. She secretly made plans to kill him to revenge Desdemona's death.

6. Who told the truth about Iago?
    A. Emilia
    B. Roderigo
    C. Desdemona
    D. Cassio

Othello - Multiple Choice Study/Quiz Questions Page 7

7. What happened to Othello?
    A. He remained in his position, remarried, and lived happily.
    B. He killed himself.
    C. He returned to his native country, prepared an army, and attacked Venice.
    D. He lost his mind and wandered around the streets. People took pity on him and fed and protected him.

8. What happened to Iago?
    A. He killed himself.
    B. He fled the country and was never heard from again.
    C. He was stabbed and imprisoned.
    D. He confessed and spent the rest of his life in a contemplative monastery, doing penance.

9. What happened to Cassio?
    A. He became the Lord Governor.
    B. He took a commission in another part of the country.
    C. He went insane from grief and finally starved to death.
    D. He married Bianca and lived a prosperous life as a private citizen.

ANSWER KEY - MULTIPLE CHOICE STUDY/QUIZ QUESTIONS
Othello

	ACT I	ACT II	ACT III	ACT IV	ACT V
1	C	A	C	B	C
2	B	C	A	A	A
3	C	C	C	B	A
4	B	D	A	B	D
5	D	A	C	C	C
6	C	B	C	A	A
7				B	B
8				C	C
9				D	A

PREREADING VOCABULARY WORKSHEETS

VOCABULARY - *Othello* : Act I

Part I: Using Prior Knowledge and Contextual Clues

Below are the sentences in which the vocabulary words appear in the text. Read the sentence. Use any clues you can find in the sentence combined with your prior knowledge, and write what you think the underlined words mean on the lines provided.

1. But he, as loing his own pride and purposes, Evades them, with a <u>bombast</u> circumstance Horribly stuffed with epithets of war.

   _____

2. 'Tis the curse of service, <u>Preferment</u> goes by letter and affection, And not by old gradation, where each second Stood heir to the first.

   _____

3. You shall mark Many a duteous and knee-crooking knave That doting on his own <u>obsequious</u> bondage Wears out his time, much like his master's ass, For naught but provender . . . .

   _____

4. My house is not a <u>grange</u>.

   _____

5. But with a knave of common hire, a gondolier, To the gross clasps of a <u>lascivious</u> Moor ---

   _____

6. If she be in her chamber or your house, Let loose on me the justice of the state For thus <u>deluding</u> you.

   _____

7. 'Tis yet to know -- Which, when I know that boasting is an honor, I shall <u>promulgate</u> -- . . . .

   _____

8. Who'er he be that in this foul proceeding Hath thus <u>beguiled</u> your daughter of herself And you of her, the bloody book of law You shall yourself read in the bitter letter . . . .

   _____

35

Ohello Vocabulary for Act I Continued

9. A natural and prompt <u>alacrity</u> I find in hardness, and do undertake These present wars against the Ottomites.

_____

Part II: Determining the Meaning - Match the vocabulary words to their dictionary definitions.

	____ 1. bombast	A. farm; grainery
	____ 2. preferment	B. deceiving
	____ 3. obsequious	C. promotion
	____ 4. grange	D. lecherous
	____ 5. lascivious	E. eagerness; quickness
	____ 6. deluding	F. puffed-up; pompous
	____ 7. promulgate	G. officially announce
	____ 8. beguiled	H. diverted; taken away; also charmed or delighted
	____ 9. alacrity	I. fawning; showing servile compliance

VOCABULARY - *Othello* : Act II

Part I: Using Prior Knowledge and Contextual Clues

Below are the sentences in which the vocabulary words appear in the text. Read the sentence. Use any clues you can find in the sentence combined with your prior knowledge, and write what you think the underlined words mean on the lines provided.

1. Therefore my hopes, not surfeited to death, Stand in bold cure.

_____

2. If after every tempest comes such calms, May the winds blow till they have wakened death!

_____

3. . . . they say base men being in love have then a nobility in their natures more than is native to them . . . .

_____

4. When the blood is made dull with the act of sport, there should be, again to inflame it and to give satiety a fresh appetite, loveliness in favor, sympathy in years, manners and beauties, all which the Moor is defective in.

_____

5. Besides, the knave is handsome, young, and hath all those requisites in him that folly and green minds look after.

_____

6. . . . and the impediment most profitably removed without the which there were no expectation of our prosperity.

_____

7. . . . Make the Moor thank me, love me, and reward me For making him egregiously an ass And practicing upon his peace and quiet Even to madness.

_____

8. It is Othello's pleasure, our noble and valiant General, that upon certain tidings now arrived, importing the mere perdition of the Turkish fleet, every man put himself into triumph -- . . . .

_____

Ohello Vocabulary for Act II Continued

II. Determining the Meaning - Match the words to their dictionary definitions.

____ 1. surfeited   A. the condition of being overfilled or overgratified
____ 2. tempest   B. total ruin; damnation
____ 3. base   C. requirements
____ 4. satiety   D. conspicuously offensively
____ 5. requisites   E. violent storm
____ 6. impediment   F. common; low in station
____ 7. egregiously   G. something in the way; a hinderance
____ 8. perdition   H. fed to excess

VOCABULARY - *Othello* : Act III

Part I: Using Prior Knowledge and Contextual Clues

Below are the sentences in which the vocabulary words appear in the text. Read the sentence. Use any clues you can find in the sentence combined with your prior knowledge, and write what you think the underlined words mean on the lines provided.

1. His bed shall seem a school, his board a shrift. I'll intermingle every thing he does With Cassio's suit.

_____

2. Whereon I do beseech thee grant me this . . . .

_____

3. Did Michael Cassio, when you wooed my lady, Know of your love?

_____

4. Thou dost conspire against thy friend, Iago . . . .

_____

5. Note if your lady strain his entertainment With any strong or vehement importunity -- Much will be seen in that.

_____

6. . . . --this hand of yours requires A sequester from liberty, fasting and prayer, much castigation, exercise devout.

_____

7. My advocation is now in tune.

_____

8. But now I find I had suborned the witness, And he's indicted falsely.

_____

Ohello Vocabulary for Act III Continued

II. Determining the Meaning - Match the words to their dictionary definitions.

____ 1. shrift   A. earnestly request
____ 2. beseech   B. repeated requests
____ 3. wooed   C. confessional
____ 4. conspire   D. induced to commit a bad action or perjury
____ 5. importunity   E. a cause or a path of action
____ 6. castigation   F. secretly plot
____ 7. advocation   G. punishment; criticism
____ 8. suborned   H. courted; dated

VOCABULARY - *Othello* : Act IV

Part I: Using Prior Knowledge and Contextual Clues

Below are the sentences in which the vocabulary words appear in the text. Read the sentence. Use any clues you can find in the sentence combined with your prior knowledge, and write what you think the underlined words mean on the lines provided.

1-2. Thus credulous fools are caught, And many worthy and chaste dames even thus, All guiltless, meet reproach.

_____

_____

3. . . . of so high and plenteous wit and invention ---

_____

4. If you are so find over her iniquity, give her patent to offend . . . .

_____

5. Get me some poison, Iago, this night. I'll not expostulate with her, lest her body and beauty unprovide my mind again.

_____

6. Sir, I obey the mandate, And will return to Venice.

_____

7. The bawdy wind, that kisses all it meets, Is hushed within the hollow mine of earth And will not hear it.

_____

8. I will be hanged if some eternal villain, Some busy and insinuating rogue, Some cogging, cozening slave, to get some office, Have not devised this slander.

_____

9. He says he will return incontinent.

_____

41

Ohello Vocabulary for Act IV Continued

II. Determining the Meaning - Match the words to their dictionary definitions.

____ 1. credulous   A. command; official instruction
____ 2. reproach   B. introducing an idea subtlely
____ 3. wit   C. criticism; disgrace; blame; shame
____ 4. iniquity   D. gullible
____ 5. expostulate   E. vulgar; humorously coarse
____ 6. mandate   F. uncontrolled; unrestrained
____ 7. bawdy   G. reason earnestly
____ 8. insinuating   H. sin(s)
____ 9. incontinent   I. intelligence; humor

VOCABULARY - *Othello* : Act V

Part I: Using Prior Knowledge and Contextual Clues
 Below are the sentences in which the vocabulary words appear in the text. Read the sentence. Use any clues you can find in the sentence combined with your prior knowledge, and write what you think the underlined words mean on the lines provided.

1. Wear thy good rapier barde, and put it home. Quick, quick, fear nothing, I'll be at thy elbow. It makes us, or it <u>mars</u> us. Think on that, And fix most firm thy resolution.

_____

2. There stand I in much <u>peril</u>.

_____

3. Nay, if you stare, we shall hear more <u>anon</u>.

_____

4. <u>Fie</u>, fie upon thee, strumpet!

_____

5. I would not have thee <u>linger</u> in thy pain.

_____

6. If he say so, may his <u>pernicious</u> soul Rot half a grain a day!

_____

7. And she did <u>gratify</u> his amorous works . . . .

_____

8. That handkerchief thou speak'st of I found by fortune and did give my husband, For often with a solemn earnestness, More than indeed belonged to such a <u>trifle</u>, He begged of me to steal it.

_____

9. Do you go back <u>dismayed</u>?

_____

Othello Vocabulary for Act V Continued

10. Speak of me as I am, nothing extenuate, Nor set down aught in <u>malice</u>.

_____

II. Determining the Meaning - Match the words to their dictionary definitions.

_____ 1. mars   A. damages; marks
_____ 2. peril   B. to be slow in learning
_____ 3. anon   C. reward; indulge; satisfy
_____ 4. fie   D. spite; ill-will
_____ 5. linger   E. something of little importance or value
_____ 6. pernicious   F. used to express distaste or disapproval
_____ 7. gratify   G. danger
_____ 8. trifle   H. having lost courage
_____ 9. dismayed   I. deadly; destructive
_____ 10. malice   J. soon

ANSWER KEY - VOCABULARY
Othello

Act I	Act II	Act III	Act IV	Act V
1. F	1. H	1. C	1. D	1. A
2. C	2. E	2. A	2. C	2. G
3. I	3. F	3. H	3. I	3. J
4. A	4. A	4. F	4. H	4. F
5. D	5. C	5. B	5. G	5. B
6. B	6. G	6. G	6. A	6. I
7. G	7. D	7. E	7. E	7. C
8. H	8. B	8. D	8. B	8. E
9. E			9. F	9. H
				10. D

DAILY LESSONS

LESSON ONE

Objectives
1. To gather background information
2. To give students the opportunity to fulfill their nonfiction reading assignment
3. To give students practice using the resources in the library
4. To distribute the materials which will be used in the unit

Activity #1
Distribute the materials which will be used in this unit. Explain in detail how students are to use these materials.

Study Guides Students should read the study guide questions for each reading assignment prior to beginning the reading assignment to get a feeling for what events and ideas are important in the section they are about to read. After reading the section, students will (as a class or individually) answer the questions to review the important events and ideas from that section of the play. Students should keep the study guides as study materials for the unit test.

Vocabulary Prior to reading a reading assignment, students will do vocabulary work related to the section of the play they are about to read. Following the completion of the reading of the play, there will be a vocabulary review of all the words used in the vocabulary assignments. Students should keep their vocabulary work as study materials for the unit test.

Reading Assignment Sheet You need to fill in the reading assignment sheet to let students know by when their reading has to be completed. You can either write the assignment sheet up on a side blackboard or bulletin board and leave it there for students to see each day, or you can "ditto" copies for each student to have. In either case, you should advise students to become very familiar with the reading assignments so they know what is expected of them.

Extra Activities Center The Extra Activities page of this unit contains suggestions for an extra library of related plays and articles in your classroom as well as crossword and word search puzzles. Make an extra activities center in your room where you will keep these materials for students to use. (Bring the books and articles in from the library and keep several copies of the puzzles on hand.) Explain to students that these materials are available for students to use when they finish reading assignments or other class work early.

Nonfiction Assignment Sheet Explain to students that they each are to read at least one non-fiction piece from the in-class library at some time during the unit. Students will fill out a nonfiction assignment sheet after completing the reading to help you evaluate their reading experiences and to help the students think about and evaluate their own reading experiences.

<u>Books</u> Each school has its own rules and regulations regarding student use of school books. Advise students of the procedures that are normal for your school.

<u>Activity #2</u>

Take students to your school library. Distribute the Research Assignment Sheet. Discuss the directions in detail, and give students ample time to complete the assignment. Depending on how quickly your students work, you may also need to spend part of the class period for Lesson Two in the library.

RESEARCH ASSIGNMENT - *Othello*

Purposes
    1. To give you some background information about Shakespeare, *Othello* and the historical era in which the play was written and performed
    2. To help you fulfill the nonfiction reading assignment which is a part of this unit

Assignment
    Use the resources of your library and/or media center to find out as much as you can about the topic your group has been assigned. Take notes so you remember what you have read, seen or heard. After you have collected your information, get together with the other members of your group to compile a "Fact Sheet," an outline of the facts you have gathered. You will be asked to give an oral report to share your information with the rest of your classmates so that everyone in your class will have information about each of the topics assigned. The "Fact Sheet" you prepare will be the basis of your oral report and, if duplicated, will serve as a study guide for you and your classmates.
    If you wish, you may use this assignment to fulfill your nonfiction reading assignment for this unit. If you choose to do so, be sure to fill out your Nonfiction Reading Assignment Sheet.

    Group 1: Research Shakespeare. Pretend as if you had to write a book about Shakespeare (a biography). Include information about his personal life, professional life, important events and influences in his life, and any topics of controversy surrounding his life.

    Group 2: Research British History 1550-1650. What was going on in Britain during the time just before, during and just after Shakespeare lived? Who were the rulers? What was the political atmosphere? What were the people concerned about? How did the people live? Answer these kinds of questions in your report.

    Group 3: Research World History 1550-1650. What was going on in the rest of the world (besides Britain) during this period?

    Group 4: Research *Othello*. What is the play about? Why is it famous? What do critics say about it? Has there been more than one version of the play? Which one(s) are most often performed? Why? Which is/was the best production of the play? What difficulties are there in performing the play (if any)?

Getting Started
    There are many sources of information for your research. Books, periodicals (magazines & journals), films/filmstrips/videos, and encyclopedias are some of the most commonly used research materials. Each member of your group should use a different source of materials. For example, one member should look for books, another should look for articles in periodicals, etc.

NONFICTION ASSIGNMENT SHEET
(To be completed after reading the required nonfiction article)

Name _____ Date _____

Title of Nonfiction Read _____

Written By _____ Publication Date _____

I. Factual Summary: Write a short summary of the piece you read.

II. Vocabulary
    1. With which vocabulary words in the piece did you encounter some degree of difficulty?

    2. How did you resolve your lack of understanding with these words?

III. Interpretation: What was the main point the author wanted you to get from reading his work?

IV. Criticism
    1. With which points of the piece did you agree or find easy to accept? Why?

    2. With which points of the piece did you disagree or find difficult to believe? Why?

V. Personal Response: What do you think about this piece? OR How does this piece influence your ideas?

LESSON TWO

Objectives
1. To give students time to finish their research
2. To give students time to compile their fact sheets
3. To evaluate students' research
4. To have students share all the information they have found

Activity #1

Give students ample time to complete their research and compile their research fact sheets.

Activity #2

Have one student from each group give an oral report to the class summarizing the information all the group members found. If you choose, students could just listen instead of taking notes, and you could duplicate the fact sheets for distribution in the next class period. The other alternative is to have students take notes from the class reports so they have study materials.

LESSON THREE

Objectives
1. To assign reading parts for Act I
2. To do the prereading activities for Act I

Activity #1
    Explain that because *Othello* is a play it is meant to be acted on a stage. If you are not planning a production of the play, explain to students that the next best thing we can do is to read the parts orally. Each person in class will (eventually) have a speaking part to perform. The part does not have to be memorized, but the students' oral reading will be evaluated.

    Make the reading part assignments for Act I, which will be read in Lesson Five. (Tell students the day and date that their reading will be done.)

Narrator (stage descriptions and directions; italicized)

Scene One	Scene Three
Roderigo	Duke
Iago	1 Sen
Brabantio	2 Sen
	Sailor
Scene Two	1 Officer
Othello	Messenger
Cassio	Desdemona
Roderigo	Roderigo
Brabantio	Iago
	Othello
	Brabantio

Activity #3
    Prior to reading Act I, students should preview the study questions and do the prereading vocabulary work for Act I. Give students the remainder of this class period to do the prereading work and, if they finish that, to begin practicing their oral reading parts.

LESSONS FOUR AND FIVE

Objectives
    1. To read Act I of *Othello*
    2. To evaluate students' oral reading

Activity
    Have students who were assigned to read parts for Act I do so during these class periods. If you have not yet evaluated students' oral reading this marking period, this would be a good opportunity to do so. An Oral Reading Evaluation form is included in this unit for your convenience.

LESSON SIX

Objectives
    1. To review the main events and ideas presented in Act I
    2. To assign the speaking parts for Act II
    3. To do the prereading work for Act II

Activity #1
    Give students a few minutes to formulate answers for the study guide questions for Act I, and then discuss the answers to the questions in detail. Write the answers on the board or overhead transparency so students can have the correct answers for study purposes. Note: It is a good practice in public speaking and leadership skills for individual students to take charge of leading the discussions of the study questions. Perhaps a different student could go to the front of the class and lead the discussion each day that the study questions are discussed during this unit. Of course, the teacher should guide the discussion when appropriate and be sure to fill in any gaps the students leave.

Activity #2
    Assign the following speaking parts for Act II. (Tell students that they will be reading Act II during the next class period.)

Narator

Scene One
Montano
1 Gent
2 Gent
3 Gent
4 Gent
Roderigo
Cassio
Desdemona
Iago
Othello

Scene Two
Herald

Scene Three
Othello
Cassio
Iago
Montano
Roderigo

Activity #3
    Prior to reading Act II, students should preview the study questions and do the prereading vocabulary work for Act II. Give students the remainder of this class period to do the prereading work and, if they finish that, to begin practicing their oral reading parts.

ORAL READING EVALUATION - *Othello*

Name _____ Class _____ Date _____

SKILL	EXCELLENT	GOOD	AVERAGE	FAIR	POOR
Fluency	5	4	3	2	1
Clarity	5	4	3	2	1
Audibility	5	4	3	2	1
Pronunciation	5	4	3	2	1
_____	5	4	3	2	1
_____	5	4	3	2	1

Total _____   Grade _____

Comments:

LESSON SEVEN

Objectives
    1. To read Act II of *Othello*
    2. To evaluate students' oral reading

Activity
    Have students who were assigned to read parts for Act II do so during these class periods. If you have not yet evaluated students' oral reading this marking period, this would be a good opportunity to do so. An Oral Reading Evaluation form is included in this unit for your convenience.

LESSON EIGHT

Objectives
    1. To give students practice writing to inform
    2. To review
    3. To give the teacher the opportunity to evaluate students' writing

Activity
    Distribute Writing Assignment 1. Discuss the directions in detail and give students this class period to do the assignment.

    Follow - Up: After you have graded the assignments, have a writing conference with the students. After the writing conference, allow students to revise their papers using your suggestions and corrections. Give them about three days from the date they receive their papers to complete the revision. I suggest grading the revisions on an A-C-E scale (all revisions well-done, some revisions made, few or no revisions made). This will speed your grading time and still give some credit for the students' efforts.

WRITING ASSIGNMENT #1 - *Othello*

PROMPT
Your assignment is to write a complete composition about the background information you researched at the beginning of this unit.

PREWRITING
Start by looking at the notes you took as you were gathering information. Then, look at the fact sheet you and the members of your group compiled. Think of one statement you could make about all this information. That will be the main idea of your paper. Can the information you have gathered be put into categories? (Are there some things that naturally go together?) Is there a logical progression of ideas? (Can your information be put in chronological order? If so, do it.)

DRAFTING
First write a paragraph in which you introduce the topic of your composition. The paragraphs in the body of your composition will all support or explain your main topic. The paragraphs should flow from idea to idea (from category to category, or in chronological order from earliest to latest, etc.). Your final paragraph should include the conclusions you can draw from the information presented and should bring your composition to a close.

PROMPT
When you finish the rough draft of your paper, ask a student who sits near you to read it. After reading your rough draft, he/she should tell you what he/she liked best about your work, which parts were difficult to understand, and ways in which your work could be improved. Reread your paper considering your critic's comments, and make the corrections you think are necessary.

PROOFREADING
Do a final proofreading of your paper double-checking your grammar, spelling, organization, and the clarity of your ideas.

LESSON NINE

Objectives
    1. To review the main events and ideas presented in Act II
    2. To assign the speaking parts for Act III
    3. To do the prereading work for Act III

Activity #1
    Give students a few minutes to formulate answers for the study guide questions for Act II, and then discuss the answers to the questions in detail. Write the answers on the board or overhead transparency so students can have the correct answers for study purposes.

Activity #2
    Assign the following speaking parts for Act III. (Tell students that they will be reading Act III during the next class period.)

Narrator

Scene One
Cassio
Clown
1 Musician
Iago
Emilia

Scene Two
Othello
Iago
Gent

Scene Three
Desdemona
Emilia
Cassio
Iago
Othello

Scene Four
Desdemona
Clown
Emilia
Othello
Iago
Bianca
Cassio

Activity #3
    Prior to reading Act III, students should preview the study questions and do the prereading vocabulary work for Act III. Give students the remainder of this class period to do the prereading work and, if they finish that, to begin practicing their oral reading parts.

LESSONS TEN AND ELEVEN

Objectives
  1. To read Act III of *Othello*
  2. To evaluate students' oral reading

Activity
  Have students who were assigned to read parts for Act III do so during these class periods. Continue the oral reading evaluations if you have not yet given everyone in the class a grade for oral reading.

LESSON TWELVE

Objectives
  1. To review the main events and ideas presented in Act III
  2. To assign the speaking parts for Act IV
  3. To do the prereading work for Act IV

Activity #1
  Give students a few minutes to formulate answers for the study guide questions for Act III, and then discuss the answers to the questions in detail. Write the answers on the board or overhead transparency so students can have the correct answers for study purposes.

Activity #2
  Assign the following speaking parts for Act IV. (Tell students that they will be reading Act IV during the next class period.)

Narrator

Scene One
Iago
Othello
Cassio
Bianca
Lodovico
Desdemona

Scene Two
Iago
Othello
Desdemona
Emilia
Roderigo

Scene Three
Othello
Emilia
Desdemona
Lodovico

Activity #3
  Prior to reading Act IV, students should preview the study questions and do the prereading vocabulary work for Act IV. Give students the remainder of this class period to do the prereading work and, if they finish that, to begin practicing their oral reading parts.

LESSON THIRTEEN

Objectives
    1. To read Act IV of *Othello*
    2. To evaluate students' oral reading

Activity
    Have students who were assigned to read parts for Act IV do so during these class periods. Continue the oral reading evaluations if you have not yet given everyone in the class a grade for oral reading.

LESSON FOURTEEN

Objectives
    1. To review the main events and ideas presented in Act IV
    2. To assign the speaking parts for Act V
    3. To do the prereading work for Act V

Activity #1
    Give students a few minutes to formulate answers for the study guide questions for Act IV, and then discuss the answers to the questions in detail. Write the answers on the board or overhead transparency so students can have the correct answers for study purposes.

Activity #2
    Assign the following speaking parts for Act V. (Tell students that they will be reading Act V during the next class period.)

Narrator	Scene Two
	Othello
Scene One	Desdemona
Iago	Emilia
Roderigo	Gratiano
Cassio	Lodovico
Othello	Iago
Gratiano	Montana
Lodovico	
Bianca	
Emilia	

Activity #3
    Prior to reading Act V, students should preview the study questions and do the prereading vocabulary work for Act V. Give students the remainder of this class period to do the prereading work and, if they finish that, to begin practicing their oral reading parts.

LESSON FIFTEEN

Objectives
1. To read Act V of *Othello*
2. To evaluate students' oral reading

Activity

Have students who were assigned to read parts for Act V do so during these class periods. Continue the oral reading evaluations if you have not yet given everyone in the class a grade for oral reading.

LESSON SIXTEEN

Objectives
1. To review the main ideas and events from Act V
2. To review all of the vocabulary work done in this unit

Activity #1

Give students a few minutes to formulate answers for the study guide questions for Act V, and then discuss the answers to the questions in detail.

Activity #2

Choose one (or more) of the vocabulary review activities listed on the next page and spend your class period as directed in the activity. Some of the materials for these review activities are located in the Vocabulary Resource section of this unit.

LESSON SEVENTEEN

Objectives
1. To give students the opportunity to practice writing to persuade
2. To give the teacher a chance to evaluate students' individual writing
3. To give students the opportunity to correct their writing errors and produce an error-free paper

Activity

Distribute Writing Assignment 2. Discuss the directions in detail and give students ample time to complete the assignment.

While students are doing their writing assignments, call individuals to your desk (or some other private area) to discuss their papers from Writing Assignment 1. A Writing Evaluation Form is included with this unit to help structure your conferences.

VOCABULARY REVIEW ACTIVITIES

1. Divide your class into two teams and have an old-fashioned spelling or definition bee.

2. Give each of your students (or students in groups of two, three or four) an *Othello* Vocabulary Word Search Puzzle. The person (group) to find all of the vocabulary words in the puzzle first wins.

3. Give students an *Othello* Vocabulary Word Search Puzzle without the word list. The person or group to find the most vocabulary words in the puzzle wins.

4. Use an *Othello* Vocabulary Crossword Puzzle. Put the puzzle onto a transparency on the overhead projector (so everyone can see it), and do the puzzle together as a class.

5. Give students an *Othello* Vocabulary Matching Worksheet to do.

6. Divide your class into two teams. Use the *Othello* vocabulary words with their letters jumbled as a word list. Student 1 from Team A faces off against Student 1 from Team B. You write the first jumbled word on the board. The first student (1A or 1B) to unscramble the word wins the chance for his/her team to score points. If 1A wins the jumble, go to student 2A and give him/her a definition. He/she must give you the correct spelling of the vocabulary word which fits that definition. If he/she does, Team A scores a point, and you give student 3A a definition for which you expect a correctly spelled matching vocabulary word. Continue giving Team A definitions until some team member makes an incorrect response. An incorrect response sends the game back to the jumbled-word face off, this time with students 2A and 2B. Instead of repeating giving definitions to the first few students of each team, continue with the student after the one who gave the last incorrect response on the team. For example, if Team B wins the jumbled-word face-off, and student 5B gave the last incorrect answer for Team B, you would start this round of definition questions with student 6B, and so on. The team with the most points wins!

7. Have students write a story in which they correctly use as many vocabulary words as possible. Have students read their compositions orally! Post the most original compositions on your bulletin board!

WRITING ASSIGNMENT #2 - *Othello*

PROMPT

We are constantly being persuaded by our friends, family members, teachers, advertisements, and many other sources. The art of persuasion is an important tool to have; if you are really good at it, you can convince most people of just about anything.

Your assignment is to rewrite Act V Scene ii having Emilia enter Desdemona's chamber *before* Othello stifles her, and have Emilia persuade Othello *not* to kill Desdemona.

PREWRITING

Make a list of arguments Emilia could use. Make a list of Othello's possible responses to each argument. What will Desdemona's reaction be? After you make lists with possible scenarios, choose the arguments and responses you think will be the best and most likely considering the characters involved.

DRAFTING

Imitate Shakespeare's writing style to write your scene. Make a rough draft of the dialogue and then go back to fine-tune it and add any necessary stage directions.

PROMPT

When you finish the rough draft of your paper, ask a student who sits near you to read it. After reading your rough draft, he/she should tell you what he/she liked best about your work, which parts were difficult to understand, and ways in which your work could be improved. Reread your paper considering your critic's comments, and make the corrections you think are necessary.

PROOFREADING

Do a final proofreading of your paper double-checking your grammar, spelling, organization, and the clarity of your ideas.

WRITING EVALUATION FORM - *Othello*

Name _____ Date _____

Grade _____

Circle One For Each Item:

Grammar:		correct		errors noted on paper

Spelling:		correct		errors noted on paper

Punctuation:		correct		errors noted on paper

Legibility:		excellent	good	fair	poor

Strengths:

Weaknesses:

Comments/Suggestions:

LESSONS EIGHTEEN AND NINETEEN

Objectives
1. To study the characters of the play more closely
2. To give students the opportunity to work in small groups to study the text, find and process information

Activity #1

Divide the class into six groups. Each group should be assigned one of the following characters:
Iago
Othello
Desdemona
Emilia
Cassio
Roderigo

Each group should look at its character through the entire play. Group members should identify their character's role in the play, give a list of important characteristics of that character, and give at least one example from the text which shows each characteristic. (For example, if they list 4 characteristics, they should have 4 examples, one for each characteristic.) The group should also report any significant character changes its character develops through the play.

Groups may subdivide, assigning one act per student to break down the work load. If they do subdivide, each student should take his own notes, and when all students are done, they should discuss and compile their information.

One group member should be designated "secretary to jot down the group's ideas. Another should be designated "spokesperson" to report the group's ideas to the class.

Activity #2

The groups will each report their findings and conclusions to the whole class. The teacher or a student should write down on the board or overhead projector all of the findings and conclusions. Students should all take notes from the board for later study.

LESSON TWENTY

Objectives
1. To discuss *Othello* on interpretive and critical levels
2. To take a closer look at Shakespeare's language and significant quotations from *Othello*

Activity

Choose the questions from the Extra Discussion Questions/Writing Assignments which seem most appropriate for your students. A class discussion of these questions is most effective if students have been given the opportunity to formulate answers to the questions prior to the discussion. To this end, you may either have all the students formulate answers to all the questions, divide your class into groups and assign one or more questions to each group, or you could assign one question to each student in your class. The option you choose will make a difference in the amount of class time needed for this activity.

After students have had ample time to formulate answers to the questions, begin your class discussion of the questions and the ideas presented by the questions. Be sure students take notes during the discussion so they have information to study for the unit test.

EXTRA WRITING ASSIGNMENTS/DISCUSSION QUESTIONS - *Othello*

<u>Interpretation</u>

1. From what point of view is *Othello* told? Why?

2. What is the setting of *Othello*?

3. Where is the climax of the play? Explain your choice.

4. How much time passes during the play?

5. Think of a different title for the play. Explain your choice.

6. What are the main conflicts in the play, and how are they resolved?

<u>Critical</u>

7. Explain why *Othello* is a tragedy.

8. Describe the relationship between Othello and Iago.

9. Are Othello's actions believably motivated? Explain why or why not.

10. Are Iago's actions believably motivated? Explain why or why not.

11. Characterize William Shakespeare's style of writing. How does it contribute to the value of the play?

12. Choose a passage from *Othello* (at least 10 lines). Analyze the meter, rhymes and word choice in relationship to the meaning and action of the passage.

13. Compare and contrast Desdemona and Emilia.

14. Describe the relationship between Desdemona and Othello.

15. Why did Othello believe Iago instead of Desdemona?

16. What was the function of Brabantio in the play?

17. How and why was Cassio a victim?

18. Describe Shakespeare's use of light and dark imagery.

19. In what ways did Desdemona's "willow" song parallel her own life?

Othello Extra Discussion Questions page 2

20. All of the characters in the play seem to like Iago through most of the play. Why?

21. Why did Shakespeare allow Cassio to live?

22. As is typical of Shakespearian characters, the characters in *Othello* often make little puns or jokes. Give several examples of these kinds of passages and explain the value of such passages.

23. Are the characters in *Othello* stereotypes? If so, explain why William Shakespeare used stereotypes. If not, explain how the characters merit individuality.

24. Discuss time in *Othello*.

Critical/Personal Response
21. Which minor character is the most important to the play? Explain why.

22. Did Iago have any redeeming qualities?

23. What do you think will happen to Iago?

24. Do you think the relationship between Othello and Desdemona is realistic? Explain why or why not.

25. Why do you think Othello killed Desdemona?

26. Why didn't Brabantio want Desdemona to marry Othello?

27. Suppose Emilia had told Desdemona about the handkerchief. What effect could that have had on future events in the play?

Personal Response
28. Did you enjoy reading *Othello*? Why or why not?

29. What would you have done if you were Othello? Would you have believed Desdemona (your spouse) or Iago (your friend)?

30. If you have read other plays by Shakespeare, tell how Othello measured up to the others you have read. Did you like it more or less or the same? Why?

Othello Extra Discussion Questions page 3

Quotations
IDENTIFY AND EXPLAIN THE FOLLOWING QUOTATIONS FROM *Othello*.

1. I am not what I am. (Ii65)

2. It seems not meet, nor wholesome to my place,
   To be produced -- as if I stay I shall --
   Against the Moor. (Ii146-148)

3. Fathers, from hence trust not your daughters' minds
   By what you see them act. (Ii171-172)

4. By Janus, I think no. (Iii33)

5. Good signior, you shall more command with years
   Than with your weapons. (Iii60-61)

6. I think this tale would win my daughter too.
   Good Brabantio,
   Take up this mangled matter at the best. (Iiii171-173)

7. So please your Grace, my Ancient,
   A man he is of honesty and trust.
   To his conveyance I assign my wife. (Iiii284-286)

8. Your son-in-law is far more fair than black. (Iiii291)

9. Look to her, Moor, if thou hast eyes to see.
   She has deceived her father, and may thee. (Iiii293-294)

Othello Extra Discussion Questions page 4

10. Let us be conjunctive in our revenge against him. (Iiii374)

11. The Moor is of a free and open nature
    That thinks men honest that but seem to be so,
    And will as tenderly be led by the nose
    As asses are. (Iiii405-408)

12. Oh, you are well tuned now,
    But I'll set down the pegs that make this music,
    As honest as I am. (IIi202-204)

13. Provoke him, that he may, for even out of that will I cause these of Cyprus to mutiny, whose qualification shall come into no true taste again but by the displanting of Cassio. (IIi279-282)

14. . . . yet that I put the Moor
    At least into a jealousy so strong
    That judgement cannot cure. (IIi309-311)

15. Knavery's plain face is never seen till used. (IIi321)

16. She's a most exquisite lady. (IIiii18)

17. If I can fasten but one cup upon him
    With that which he hath drunk tonight already
    He'll be as full of quarrel and offense
    As my young mistress' dog. (IIiii50-53)

18. And 'tis great pity that the noble Moor
    Should hazard such a place as his own second
    With one of an ingraft infirmity. (IIiii143-145)

Othello Extra Discussion Questions page 5

19. I had rather have this tongue cut from my mouth
    Than it should do offense to Michael Cassio.
    Yet I persuade myself to speak the truth
    Shall nothing wrong him. (IIiii221-224)

20. I know, Iago
    Thy honesty and love doth mince this matter,
    Making it light to Cassio. (IIiii247-249)

21. Reputation, reputation, reputation! Oh, I have lost my reputation! I have lost the immortal part of myself, and what remains is bestial. My reputation, Iago, my reputation! (IIiii262-265)

22. Our General's wife is now the General. (IIiii320)

23. Confess yourself freely to her, importune her help to put you in your place again. (IIiii322-323)

24. And what's he then that says I play the villain? (IIiii342)

25. So will I turn her virtue into pitch,
    And out of her won goodness make the net
    That shall enmesh them all. (IIiii366-368)

26. No, sure, I cannot think it,
    That he would steal away so guilty-like,
    Seeing you coming. (IIIiii37-39)

Othello Extra Discussion Questions page 6

27. Men should be what they seem,
   Or those that be not, would they might seem none! (IIIiii127-128)

28. Utter my thoughts? Why, say they are vile and false (IIIiii136)

29. No, Iago,
   I'll see before I doubt, when I doubt, prove,
   And on the proof, there is no more but this --
   Away at once with love or jealousy! (IIIiii189-192)

30. I do not think but Desdemona's honest. (IIIiii225)

31. Why did I marry? This honest creature doubtless
   Sees and knows more, much more, than he unfolds. (IIIiii242-243)

32. Do not chide, I have a thing for you. (IIIiii301)

33. Trifles light as air
   Are to the jealous confirmations strong
   As proofs of Holy Writ. (IIIiii322-324)

34. Oh, now forever
   Farewell the tranquil mind! Farewell content! (IIIiii347-348)

35. Farewell! Othello's occupation's gone! (IIIiii357)

36. I think my wife be honest, and think she is not.
   I think that thou art just, and think thou are not.
   I'll have some proof. (IIIiii384-386)

Othello Extra Discussion Questions page 7

37. I know not, madam. (IIIiv24)

38. There's magic in the web of it. (IIIiv69)

39. They are not ever jealous for the cause,
   But jealous for they are jealous. 'Tis a monster
   Begot upon itself, born on itself. (IIIiv160-162)

40. Her honor is an essence that's not seen.
   They have it very oft that have it not. (IVi16-17)

41. Work on,
   My medicine, work! Thus credulous fools are caught,
   And many worthy and chaste dames even thus,
   All guiltless, meet reproach. (IVi45-48)

42. For I will make him tell the tale anew,
   Where, how, how oft, how long ago, and when
   He hath and is again to cope your wife. (IVi86-87)

43. If that the earth could teem with a woman's tears,
   Each drop she falls would prove a crocodile. (IVi256-257)

44. If any wretch have put this in your head,
   Let Heaven requite it with the serpent's curse! (IVii15-16)

45. Oh, thou weed,
   Who art so lovely and fair and smell'st so sweet
   That the sense aches at thee, would thou hadst ne'er been born! (IVii67-69)

Othello Extra Discussion Questions page 8

46. If any such there be, Heaven pardon him!
    A halter pardon him! And Hell gnaw his bones! (IVii135-136)

47. Faith, I have heard too much, for your words and performances are no kin together. (IVii184-185)

48. The world is a huge thing. It is a great price
    For a small vice. (IViii68-69)

49. The ills we do, their ills instruct us so. (IViii103)

50. Now, whether he kill Cassio,
    Or Cassio him, or each do kill the other,
    Every way makes my gain. (Vi12-14)

51. Oh, damned Iago! Oh, inhuman dog! (Vi63)

52. This is the night
    That either makes me or fordoes me quite. (Vi128-129)

53. Yet she must die, else she'll betray more men.
    Put out the light, and then put out the light.
    If I quench thee, thou flaming minister,
    I can again thy former light restore,
    Should I repent me. (Vii6-9)

54. I would not kill thy unprepared spirit. (Vii31)

Othello Extra Discussion Questions page 9

55. Nobody, I myself. Farewell. (V.ii.124)

56. I told him what I thought, and told no more
    Than what he found himself was apt and true. (V.ii.176-177)

57. Oh! Oh! Oh! (V.ii.198)

58. Let Heaven and men and devils, let them all,
    All, all, cry shame against me, yet I'll speak. (V.ii.221-222)

59. But why should honor outlive honesty!
    Let it go all. (V.ii.245-246)

60. For naught did I in hate, but all in honor. (V.ii.295)

61. Then must you speak
    Of one that loved not wisely but too well,
    Of one not easily jealous, but, being wrought,
    Perplexed in the extreme, of one whose hand,
    Like the base Indian, threw a pearl away
    Richer than all his tribe -- (V.ii.343-347)

LESSON TWENTY-ONE

Objectives
1. To give students the opportunity to do some creative writing with their own ideas
2. To extend students' knowledge of the characters and events in *Othello*
3. To give the teacher a chance to evaluate students' individual writing
4. To give students the opportunity to correct their writing errors and produce an error-free paper

Activity

Distribute Writing Assignment #3. Discuss the directions orally in detail. Allow the remaining class time for students to complete the activity.

If students do not have enough class time to finish, the papers may be collected at the beginning of the next class period.

Follow-Up: Follow up as in Writing Assignment 1, allowing students to correct their errors and turn in the revision for credit. A good time for your next writing conferences would be the day following the unit test.

WRITING ASSIGNMENT #3 - *Othello*

PROMPT

You and I know Desdemona was innocent--she was "framed" by Iago. Who is responsible for Desdemona's death? Iago for framing her? Othello for committing the murder? Desdemona for not putting up more of a fight? Cassio? Which character in the play should be held accountable for her death? Write a composition in which you give your opinion as an answer to that question.

PREWRITING

Who would you put on trial for Desdemona's murder? Think about it. When you arrive at an answer, write down that person's name. Under the person's name, jot down several good reasons why you chose that person as the most responsible party. Next to each reason, give several examples from the text supporting your statement.

DRAFTING

Write an introductory paragraph in which you introduce the idea that ___ is responsible for Desdemona's death.

In the body of your composition, write a paragraph for each of the reasons you listed. Use a topic sentence for each paragraph and fill out each paragraph with the examples that support your statements.

Write a paragraph in which you give your conclusions and bring your composition to a close.

PROMPT

When you finish the rough draft of your paper, ask a student who sits near you to read it. After reading your rough draft, he/she should tell you what he/she liked best about your work, which parts were difficult to understand, and ways in which your work could be improved. Reread your paper considering your critic's comments, and make the corrections you think are necessary.

PROOFREADING

Do a final proofreading of your paper double-checking your grammar, spelling, organization, and the clarity of your ideas.

LESSON TWENTY-TWO

Objectives
1. To bring the *Othello* unit to a close
2. To tie together all the ideas and analyses for the unit
3. To give students a look at the play *Othello* because plays are meant to be seen and heard and acted out

Activity

The best thing to do is to take students to see a production of *Othello*. If however, that is impossible, find a film of the play and show it to your students. Tell students to bear in mind everything they have learned about *Othello* as they view the film.

If you have students whose minds will wander instead of watching the film, tell your students to keep a little written list of things comparing and contrasting the film with your text and their expectations.

LESSON TWENTY-THREE

Objective
To review the main ideas presented in *Othello*

Activity #1
Choose one of the review games/activities included in the packet and spend your class period as outlined there. Some materials for these activities are located in the Extra Activities Packet section of this unit.

Activity #2
Remind students that the Unit Test will be in the next class meeting. Stress the review of the Study Guides and their class notes as a last minute, brush-up review for homework.

REVIEW GAMES/ACTIVITIES - *Othello*

1. Ask the class to make up a unit test for *Othello*. The test should have 4 sections: matching, true/false, short answer, and essay. Students may use 1/2 period to make the test and then swap papers and use the other 1/2 class period to take a test a classmate has devised. (open book) You may want to use the unit test included in this packet or take questions from the students' unit tests to formulate your own test.

2. Take 1/2 period for students to make up true and false questions (including the answers). Collect the papers and divide the class into two teams. Draw a big tic-tac-toe board on the chalk board. Make one team X and one team O. Ask questions to each side, giving each student one turn. If the question is answered correctly, that students' team's letter (X or O) is placed in the box. If the answer is incorrect, no mark is placed in the box. The object is to get three marks in a row like tic-tac-toe. You may want to keep track of the number of games won for each team.

3. Take 1/2 period for students to make up questions (true/false and short answer). Collect the questions. Divide the class into two teams. You'll alternate asking questions to individual members of teams A & B (like in a spelling bee). The question keeps going from A to B until it is correctly answered, then a new question is asked. A correct answer does not allow the team to get another question. Correct answers are +2 points; incorrect answers are -1 point.

4. Have students pair up and quiz each other from their study guides and class notes.

5. Give students a *Othello* crossword puzzle to complete.

6. Divide your class into two teams. Use the *Othello* crossword words with their letters jumbled as a word list. Student 1 from Team A faces off against Student 1 from Team B. You write the first jumbled word on the board. The first student (1A or 1B) to unscramble the word wins the chance for his/her team to score points. If 1A wins the jumble, go to student 2A and give him/her a clue. He/she must give you the correct word which matches that clue. If he/she does, Team A scores a point, and you give student 3A a clue for which you expect another correct response. Continue giving Team A clues until some team member makes an incorrect response. An incorrect response sends the game back to the jumbled-word face off, this time with students 2A and 2B. Instead of repeating giving clues to the first few students of each team, continue with the student after the one who gave the last incorrect response on the team. For example, if Team B wins the jumbled-word face-off, and student 5B gave the last incorrect answer for Team B, you would start this round of clue questions with student 6B, and so on. The team with the most points wins!

UNIT TESTS

SHORT ANSWER UNIT TEST 1 - *Othello*

I. Matching/Identify

____ 1. Bianca   A. Tells of the letters found in Roderigo's pockets

____ 2. Emilia   B. Othello's wife

____ 3. Desdemona   C. The jealous Moor

____ 4. Roderigo   D. Iago's wife

____ 5. Iago   E. Brother of Brabantio

____ 6. Cassio   F. Cassio's mistress

____ 7. Othello   G. Desdemona's father

____ 8. Lodovico   H. He was passed over for a promotion

____ 9. Gratiano   I. Othello thought he was having an affair with Desdemona

____ 10. Brabantio   J. He is love-sick for Desdemona

II. Short Answer

1. What was Iago's complaint in Scene I?

2. What was Roderigo's complaint, and what was Iago's reply to it?

3. Why did Othello strip Cassio of his rank?

Othello Short Answer Unit Test 1 Page 2

4. Why did Iago want Cassio to ask Desdemona for help in restoring Othello's faith in Cassio?

5. What did Othello decide and command at the end of Scene III?

6. How did Iago trick Othello into thinking Cassio was gloating and bragging about his affair with Desdemona?

7. How did Bianca's return with the handkerchief help Iago?

8. To whom does Desdemona turn for help after Othello calls her a strumpet?

9. How would Iago gain from Roderigo's death? Cassio's?

10. Who told the truth about Iago?

Othello Short Answer Unit Test 1 Page 3

III. Quotations: Explain <u>in detail</u> the significance of ten of the following quotations.

1. I am not what I am. (Ii65)

2. So please your Grace, my Ancient,
   A man he is of honesty and trust.
   To his conveyance I assign my wife. (Iiii284-286)

3. Let us be conjunctive in our revenge against him. (Iiii374)

4. . . . yet that I put the Moor
   At least into a jealousy so strong
   That judgement cannot cure. (IIi309-311)

5. If I can fasten but one cup upon him
   With that which he hath drunk tonight already
   He'll be as full of quarrel and offense
   As my young mistress' dog. (IIiii50-53)

6. I had rather have this tongue cut from my mouth
   Than it should do offense to Michael Cassio.
   Yet I persuade myself to speak the truth
   Shall nothing wrong him. (IIiii221-224)

Othello Short Answer Unit Test 1 Page 4

7. Confess yourself freely to her, importune her help to put you in your place again. (IIiii322-323)

8. No, sure, I cannot think it,
   That he would steal away so guilty-like,
   Seeing you coming. (IIIiii37-39)

9. I do not think but Desdemona's honest. (IIIiii225)

10. Do not chide, I have a thing for you. (IIIiii301)

11. Trifles light as air
    Are to the jealous confirmations strong
    As proofs of Holy Writ. (IIIiii322-324)

12. They are not ever jealous for the cause,
    But jealous for they are jealous. 'Tis a monster
    Begot upon itself, born on itself. (IIIiv160-162)

13. Now, whether he kill Cassio,
    Or Cassio him, or each do kill the other,
    Every way makes my gain. (Vi12-14)

Othello Short Answer Unit Test 1 Page 5

14. Oh, damned Iago! Oh, inhuman dog! (Vi63)

15. I told him what I thought, and told no more
    Than what he found himself was apt and true. (Vii176-177)

16. For naught did I in hate, but all in honnor. (Vii295)

17. Then must you speak
    Of one that loved not wisely but too well,
    Of one not easily jealous, but, being wrought,
    Perplexed in the extreme, of one whose hand,
    Like the base Indian, threw a pearl away
    Richer than all his tribe -- (Vii343-347)

Othello Short Answer Unit Test 1 Page 6

IV. Vocabulary

> Listen to the vocabulary word and spell it. After you have spelled all the words, go back and write down the definition.

1.

2.

3.

4.

5.

6.

7.

8.

9.

10.

SHORT ANSWER UNIT TEST 2 - *Othello*

I. Matching

____ 1. Bianca A. Desdemona's father

____ 2. Emilia B. He is love-sick for Desdemona

____ 3. Desdemona C. Cassio's mistress

____ 4. Roderigo D. Othello thought he was having an affair with Desdemona

____ 5. Iago E. Tells of the letters found in Roderigo's pockets

____ 6. Cassio F. The jealous Moor

____ 7. Othello G. He was passed over for a promotion

____ 8. Lodovico H. Brother of Brabantio

____ 9. Gratiano I. Iago's wife

____ 10. Brabantio J. Othello's wife

II. Short Answer

1. What did Iago do to Othello? Why?

2. Why did Roderigo join Iago?

Othello Short Answer Unit Test 2 Page 2

3. What was Cassio's role in Iago's plan?

4. Why did Iago want Cassio to ask Desdemona for help in restoring Othello's faith in Cassio?

5. What was the role of the handkerchief in Iago's plan?

6. Why did Othello take Iago's word about so many things?

7. Why did Iago tell Roderigo to kill Cassio? Why did Roderigo consent to think about it?

8. What happened when Cassio and Roderigo fought?

9. What was Emilia's reaction when Othello told her that Iago had revealed Desdemona's affair with Cassio to him?

10. Who told the truth about Iago?

Othello Short Answer Unit Test 2 Page 3

III. Quotations - Explain the significance of each of the following quotations:

1. I am not what I am. (Ii65)

2. So please your Grace, my Ancient,
   A man he is of honesty and trust.
   To his conveyance I assign my wife. (Iiii284-286)

3. I do not think but Desdemona's honest. (IIIiii225)

4. Now, whether he kill Cassio,
   Or Cassio him, or each do kill the other,
   Every way makes my gain. (Vi12-14)

5. Oh, damned Iago! Oh, inhuman dog! (Vi63)

6. I told him what I thought, and told no more
   Than what he found himself was apt and true. (Vii176-177)

7. For naught did I in hate, but all in honor. (Vii295)

Othello Short Answer Unit Test 2 Page 4

IV. Vocabulary

Listen to the vocabulary word and spell it. After you have spelled all the words, go back and write down the definition.

1.

2.

3.

4.

5.

6.

7.

8.

9.

10.

KEY: SHORT ANSWER UNIT TESTS - *Othello*

The short answer questions are taken directly from the study guides.
If you need to look up the answers, you will find them in the study guide section.

Answers to the composition questions will vary depending on your
class discussions and the level of your students.

For the vocabulary section of the test, choose ten of the
words from the vocabulary lists to read orally for your students.

The answers to the matching section of the test are below.

Answers to the matching section of the Advanced Short Answer Unit Test
are the same as for Short Answer Unit Test #2.

<u>Test #1</u>
1. F
2. D
3. B
4. J
5. H
6. I
7. C
8. A
9. E
10. G

<u>Test #2</u>
1. C
2. I
3. J
4. B
5. G
6. D
7. F
8. E
9. H
10. A

ADVANCED SHORT ANSWER UNIT TEST - *Othello*

I. Matching

____ 1. Bianca   A. Desdemona's father

____ 2. Emilia   B. He is love-sick for Desdemona

____ 3. Desdemona   C. Cassio's mistress

____ 4. Roderigo   D. Othello thought he was having an affair with Desdemona

____ 5. Iago   E. Tells of the letters found in Roderigo's pockets

____ 6. Cassio   F. The jealous Moor

____ 7. Othello   G. He was passed over for a promotion

____ 8. Lodovico   H. Brother of Brabantio

____ 9. Gratiano   I. Iago's wife

____ 10. Brabantio   J. Othello's wife

II. Short Answer

1. Explain why *Othello* is a tragedy.

2. Describe the relationship between Othello and Iago.

Othello Advanced Short Answer Unit Test Page 2

3. Compare and contrast Desdemona and Emilia.

4. Why did Shakespeare allow Cassio and Iago to live?

5. Explain the importance of jealousy and revenge in *Othello*.

6. Explain the importance of loyalty and honor in *Othello*.

7. The theme of things not being as they appear to be runs rampant through *Othello*. Give at least two examples.

Othello Advanced Short Answer Unit Test Page 3

III. Composition

    Choose one quotation from *Othello* that is the most significant quotation from the play in terms of theme, plot, and characterization. Write down the quotation and defend your choice.

Othello Advanced Short Answer Unit Test Page 4

IV. Vocabulary

Listen and write down the words given. Go back later and write a composition using all of the vocabulary words. The composition must relate in some way to *Othello*.

MULTIPLE CHOICE UNIT TEST 1 - *Othello*

I. Matching

____ 1. Bianca   A. Tells of the letters found in Roderigo's pockets

____ 2. Emilia   B. Othello's wife

____ 3. Desdemona   C. The jealous Moor

____ 4. Roderigo   D. Iago's wife

____ 5. Iago   E. Brother of Brabantio

____ 6. Cassio   F. Cassio's mistress

____ 7. Othello   G. Desdemona's father

____ 8. Lodovico   H. He was passed over for a promotion

____ 9. Gratiano   I. Othello thought he was having an affair with Desdemona

____ 10. Brabantio   J. He is love-sick for Desdemona

II. Multiple Choice

1. What was Iago's complaint in Scene 1?
    A. Another officer of the same rank was receiving higher pay.
    B. Roderigo cheated during a card game and won.
    C. Cassio got the promotion that he wanted.
    D. He doesn't like the new uniforms that Othello has chosen. He thinks they make the soldiers look like weak women.

2. What was Iago's reply to Roderigo's complaint?
    A. He told Roderigo to straighten up and act like a soldier.
    B. He told Roderigo to forgive and forget.
    C. He told Roderigo they would work together for revenge.
    D. He told Roderigo to pray to the gods for guidance, then to do whatever they suggested.

Othello Multiple Choice Unit Test 1 Page 2

3. What was the result of Iago's crafty explanation of Cassio's fight with Roderigo?
    A. Othello stripped Cassio of his rank.
    B. They were both put in jail for a month.
    C. Roderigo was banished from the city for a month.
    D. Othello branded them all as troublemakers and refused to listen to them.

4. Why did Iago want Cassio to ask Desdemona for help in restoring Othello's faith in Cassio?
    A. He feels remorse for what he has done.
    B. If she would take up Cassio's cause, it would appear as though she would favor him. That would advance Iago's plot to make Othello jealous beyond reason.
    C. Iago has been secretly plotting with the Ottoman to overthrow the present government. He thinks that if he can weaken the ranks by having them worry about personal problems, the Ottomans will have a better chance of winning the war.
    D. Brabantio has offered to pay him a large sum of money to break up the marriage.

5. What did Othello decide and command at the end of Scene III?
    A. Iago was to have Cassio killed within three days. Othello would kill Desdemona himself. Iago was promoted to Lieutenant.
    B. Othello would kill Cassio, then hold Desdemona's father hostage to force her to be faithful.
    C. Othello would banish Cassio. Then Iago would pretend to be sympathetic to Desdemona. While she confessed her feelings to him, Othello would be concealed close-by. He would find them, and accuse Desdemona of being unfaithful, and imprison her.
    D. Iago would kill Cassio and Desdemona, making it look like a lover's quarrel.

6. Othello observes Iago and Cassio talking. Who does he think Cassio is talking about?
    A. Desdemona
    B. Bianca
    C. Emilia
    D. Roderigo

7. What was the effect of Bianca's returning with the handkerchief?
    A. Bianca showed her true love for Cassio.
    B. Othello believed Lago's story even more.
    C. Cassio knew then that Desdemona truly loved him.
    D. Iago's plans ere destroyed.

8. To whom does Desdemona turn for help after Othello calls her a strumpet?
    A. Cassio
    B. Emilia
    C. Iago
    D. Lodovico

Othello Multiple Choice Unit Test 1 Page 3

9. How would Iago gain from Roderigo's death?
    A. His lies to Othello would never be challenged.
    B. His relationship with Desdemona would never be revealed.
    C. He would never have to admit to stealing the jewels.
    D. Roderigo would never tell Cassio about his plot.

10. Who told the truth about Iago?
    A. Emilia
    B. Roderigo
    C. Desdemona
    D. Cassio

Othello Multiple Choice Unit Test 1 Page 4

III. Quotations - Choose the correct explanation of the following quotes:

1. I am not what I am. (Ii65)
    a. Othello is telling Iago that he is not his usual self because of the jealousy he feels towards Cassio. He hasn't been acting rationally.
    b. Othello is talking to Desdemona. He is telling her that he has lost his identity because of her infidelity. He thought his life was in order: he had a good job and a new wife, and everything seemed fine. Now he realizes that it all has been false.
    c. Iago is telling Roderigo that although he acts like a friend to Othello, he is really Othello's worst enemy sworn to revenge.
    d. Cassio is talking in a soliloquy just after he finds out that he, also, has been a victim of Iago's plot. He cannot believe that Othello thinks he is having an affair with Desdemona. He wonders what to do about his dual situation with Othello--he is not what Othello thinks he is.

2. So please your Grace, my Ancient,
   A man he is of honesty and trust.
   To his conveyance I assign my wife. (Iiii284-286)
    a. It shows Othello's total confidence in Iago, and foreshadows, ironically, that Desdemona's future lies in Iago's hands.
    b. It shows Iago's outward professions of loyalty and faith to Othello; he says he trusts Othello with all of his posession--even his wife. He knows that Othello will behave honorably.
    c. It shows Othello's total confidence in Cassio. He doesn't yet suspect that Cassio and his wife are having an affair, and that having them travel together is just what they would want.
    d. It shows Othello's confidence in Roderigo. He doesn't know that Roderigo loves Desdemona and secretly wishes for her to be his own wife. It is ironic that Othello places Desdemona in Roderigo's care just after Roderigo has agreed to join in Iago's plans for revenge.

3. I do not think but Desdemona's honest. (IIIiii225)
    a. Othello is denying Iago's charges that Desdemona is having an affair.
    b. Emilia is professing her belief that Desdemona is not having an affair.
    c. Iago is planting the idea that Desdemona may be having an affair.
    d. Cassio is trying to explain the handkerchief situation to Bianca. He knows he didn't get it from Desdemona, but he can't figure out what's going on.

Othello Multiple Choice Unit Test 1 Page 5

4. Now, whether he kill Cassio,
   Or Cassio him, or each do kill the other,
   Every way makes my gain. (Vi12-14)
   - a. Othello has discovered Iago's plan, divulged it to Cassio, and has sent Cassio to fight it out with Iago. Whether Cassio or Iago wins or both are killed, Othello is rid of either a possible suitor to his wife and/or a disgruntled subordinate who had plotted to ruin him. Either way, he wins.
   - b. Othello has sent Cassio to fight with Roderigo. He thinks Cassio is a drunken, irresponsible fool and would just as well be rid of him. He knows Roderigo is in love with Desdemona and will be a threat to him at some future date. Othello doesn't care which one wins or if they both die; he'll be glad to be rid of either one of them.
   - c. Iago has enraged Othello to the point that Othello has gone off to kill Cassio for having an affair with Desdemona. Iago doesn't care who wins, either way, he'll either complete his revenge on Othello or be rid of one person who can prove he has been lying.
   - d. Iago doesn't care whether Roderigo kills Cassio or Cassio kills Roderigo or both die. Either way he'll win; he'll either be rid of one person who knows his plan for revenge or one person who can prove he has been lying.

5. Oh, damned Iago! Oh, inhuman dog! (Vi63)
   - a. Othello has just realized Iago has been lying to him and that he has just killed innocent Desdemona.
   - b. Emilia has just realized that Iago set up the whole big lie that caused Othello to kill sweet Desdemona.
   - c. Cassio has just realized that he has been a victim of Iago's scheme.
   - d. These were Roderigo's last words before Iago finished him off.

6. I told him what I thought, and told no more
   Than what he found himself was apt and true. (Vii176-177)
   - a. Iago is defending his words to Roderigo.
   - b. Iago is defending his words to Othello.
   - c. Desdemona is explaining her conversation with Othello.
   - d. Brabantio is defending his words to Othello.

7. For naught did I in hate, but all in honnor. (Vii295)
   - a. The speaker is Iago.
   - b. The speaker is Roderigo.
   - c. The speaker is Othello.
   - d. The speaker is Emilia.

III. Composition
    Explain the roles of jealousy, revenge, loyalty and honor in *Othello*.

Othello Multiple Choice Unit Test 1 Page 7

IV. Vocabulary

____ 1. LINGER   A. To be slow in leaving

____ 2. SATIETY   B. Lecherous

____ 3. BASE   C. Danger

____ 4. INIQUITY   D. Gullible

____ 5. INCONTINENT   E. Conspicuously offensively

____ 6. SUBORNED   F. Confessional

____ 7. TEMPEST   G. Induced to commit a bad action or perjury

____ 8. WOOED   H. Violent storm

____ 9. LASCIVIOUS   I. Common; low in station

____ 10. EXPOSTULATE   J. Something of little importance or value

____ 11. IMPEDIMENT   K. Reason earnestly

____ 12. CREDULOUS   L. Fed to excess

____ 13. PERIL   M. Something in the way; a hinderance

____ 14. SHRIFT   N. Deceiving

____ 15. TRIFLE   O. Total ruin; damnation

____ 16. PERDITION   P. Sin(s)

____ 17. SURFEITED   Q. The condition of being over-filled or over-gratified

____ 18. INSINUATING   R. Uncontrolled; unrestrained

____ 19. DELUDING   S. Courted; dated

____ 20. EGREGIOUSLY   T. Introducing an idea subtlely

MULTIPLE CHOICE UNIT TEST 2 - *Othello*

I. Matching

____ 1. Bianca   A. Desdemona's father

____ 2. Emilia   B. He is love-sick for Desdemona

____ 3. Desdemona   C. Cassio's mistress

____ 4. Roderigo   D. Othello thought he was having an affair with Desdemona

____ 5. Iago   E. Tells of the letters found in Roderigo's pockets

____ 6. Cassio   F. The jealous Moor

____ 7. Othello   G. He was passed over for a promotion

____ 8. Lodovico   H. Brother of Brabantio

____ 9. Gratiano   I. Iago's wife

____ 10. Brabantio   J. Othello's wife

II. Multiple Choice

1. Brabantio complains to the Duke about Othello's marriage to Desdemona. After listening to both sides of the story, what was the Duke's reply?
    A. He agrees to annul the marriage.
    B. He remains impartial, saying a man's personal life is his own business.
    C. He reprimands Brabantio for being a petty gossip and troublemaker.
    D. He says he thinks Othello would win his daughter under the same circumstances, and tells Brabantio to make the best of the situation.

2. What was the purpose of Iago's plan?
    A. to ruin the relationship between Desdemona and Cassio
    B. to make Desdemona jealous
    C. to ruin Othello's relationship with Desdemona
    D. to make Roderigo jealous

3. What was the result of Iago's crafty explanation of Cassio's fight with Roderigo?
    A. Othello stripped Cassio of his rank.
    B. They were both put in jail for a month.
    C. Roderigo was banished from the city for a month.
    D. Othello branded them all as troublemakers and refused to listen to them.

Othello Multiple Choice Unit Test 2 Page 2

4. Why did Iago want Cassio to ask Desdemona for help in restoring Othello's faith in Cassio?
   A. He feels remorse for what he has done.
   B. If she would take up Cassio's cause, it would appear as though she would favor him. That would advance Iago's plot to make Othello jealous beyond reason.
   C. Iago has been secretly plotting with the Ottoman to overthrow the present government. He thinks that if he can weaken the ranks by having them worry about personal problems, the Ottomans will have a better chance of winning the war.
   D. Brabantio has offered to pay him a large sum of money to break up the marriage.

5. What was the effect of Bianca's returning with the handkerchief?
   A. Bianca showed her true love for Cassio.
   B. Othello believed Iago's story even more.
   C. Cassio knew then that Desdemona truly loved him.
   D. Iago's plans ere destroyed.

6. Why did Othello hit Desdomona?
   A. She had lied to him.
   B. She had tried to poison him.
   C. She had openly stated her love for Cassio.
   D. She slapped him in the face.

7. What happened when Cassio and Roderigo fought?
   A. Roderigo was wounded by Cassio. Cassio was wounded from behind by Iago.
   B. They killed each other.
   C. Iago wounded Roderigo and accidentally killed Cassio.
   D. Cassio wounded Roderigo. Roderigo wounded Cassio.

8. What was Emilia's reaction when Othello told her that Iago had revealed Desdemona's affair with Cassio?
   A. She said she had suspected it all along. She was glad it had finally come out in the open.
   B. She covered her ears and refused to listen.
   C. She was shocked and amazed. All along she thought the tale had been a lie contrived by some awful person; never dreaming that Iago was responsible.
   D. Although she publicly supported her husband, she was furious with him. She secretly made plans to kill him to revenge Desdemona's death.

9. Who told the truth about Iago?
   A. Emilia
   B. Roderigo
   C. Desdemona
   D. Cassio

Othello Multiple Choice Unit Test 2 Page 3

10. What happened to Othello?
    A. He remained in his position, remarried, and lived happily.
    B. He killed himself.
    C. He returned to his native country, prepared an army, and attacked Venice.
    D. He lost his mind and wandered around the streets. People took pity on him and fed and protected him.

Othello Multiple Choice Unit Test 2 Page 4

III. Quotations - Choose the correct explanation of the following quotes:

1. I am not what I am. (Ii65)
    a. Othello is telling Iago that he is not his usual self because of the jealousy he feels towards Cassio. He hasn't been acting rationally.
    b. Othello is talking to Desdemona. He is telling her that he has lost his identity because of her infidelity. He thought his life was in order: he had a good job and a new wife, and everything seemed fine. Now he realizes that it all has been false.
    c. Cassio is talking in a soliloquy just after he finds out that he, also, has been a victim of Iago's plot. He cannot believe that Othello thinks he is having an affair with Desdemona. He wonders what to do about his dual situation with Othello--he is not what Othello thinks he is.
    d. Iago is telling Roderigo that although he acts like a friend to Othello, he is really Othello's worst enemy sworn to revenge.

2. So please your Grace, my Ancient,
   A man he is of honesty and trust.
   To his conveyance I assign my wife. (Iiii284-286)
    a. It shows Iago's outward professions of loyalty and faith to Othello; he says he trusts Othello with all of his posession--even his wife. He knows that Othello will behave honorably.
    b. It shows Othello's total confidence in Iago, and foreshadows, ironically, that Desdemona's future lies in Iago's hands.
    c. It shows Othello's total confidence in Cassio. He doesn't yet suspect that Cassio and his wife are having an affair, and that having them travel together is just what they would want.
    d. It shows Othello's confidence in Roderigo. He doesn't know that Roderigo loves Desdemona and secretly wishes for her to be his own wife. It is ironic that Othello places Desdemona in Roderigo's care just after Roderigo has agreed to join in Iago's plans for revenge.

3. I do not think but Desdemona's honest. (IIIiii225)
    a. Iago is planting the idea that Desdemona may be having an affair.
    b. Emilia is professing her belief that Desdemona is not having an affair.
    c. Othello is denying Iago's charges that Desdemona is having an affair.
    d. Cassio is trying to explain the handkerchief situation to Bianca. He knows he didn't get it from Desdemona, but he can't figure out what's going on.

Othello Multiple Choice Unit Test 2 Page 5

4. Now, whether he kill Cassio,
   Or Cassio him, or each do kill the other,
   Every way makes my gain. (Vi12-14)
   - a. Othello has discovered Iago's plan, divulged it to Cassio, and has sent Cassio to fight it out with Iago. Whether Cassio or Iago wins or both are killed, Othello is rid of either a possible suitor to his wife and/or a disgruntled subordinate who had plotted to ruin him. Either way, he wins.
   - b. Othello has sent Cassio to fight with Roderigo. He thinks Cassio is a drunken, irresponsible fool and would just as well be rid of him. He knows Roderigo is in love with Desdemona and will be a threat to him at some future date. Othello doesn't care which one wins or if they both die; he'll be glad to be rid of either one of them.
   - c. Iago doesn't care whether Roderigo kills Cassio or Cassio kills Roderigo or both die. Either way he'll win; he'll either be rid of one person who knows his plan for revenge or one person who can prove he has been lying.
   - d. Iago has enraged Othello to the point that Othello has gone off to kill Cassio for having an affair with Desdemona. Iago doesn't care who wins, either way, he'll either complete his revenge on Othello or be rid of one person who can prove he has been lying.

5. Oh, damned Iago! Oh, inhuman dog! (Vi63)
   - a. These were Roderigo's last words before Iago finished him off.
   - b. Emilia has just realized that Iago set up the whole big lie that caused Othello to kill sweet Desdemona.
   - c. Cassio has just realized that he has been a victim of Iago's scheme.
   - d. Othello has just realized Iago has been lying to him and that he has just killed innocent Desdemona.

6. I told him what I thought, and told no more
   Than what he found himself was apt and true. (Vii176-177)
   - a. Iago is defending his words to Roderigo.
   - b. Desdemona is explaining her conversation with Othello.
   - c. Iago is defending his words to Othello.
   - d. Brabantio is defending his words to Othello.

7. For naught did I in hate, but all in honnor. (Vii295)
   - a. The speaker is Othello.
   - b. The speaker is Roderigo.
   - c. The speaker is Iago.
   - d. The speaker is Emilia.

Othello Multiple Choice Unit Test 2 Page 6

III. Composition
    Make a case for either Othello or Iago as the main character of the play.

Othello Multiple Choice Unit Test 2 Page 6

IV. Vocabulary

____ 1. MARS   A. Violent storm

____ 2. WIT   B. Eagerness; quickness

____ 3. REPROACH   C. Having lost courage

____ 4. CONSPIRE   D. Fed to excess

____ 5. SURFEITED   E. Reward; indulge; satisfy

____ 6. TEMPEST   F. Deceiving

____ 7. PREFERMENT   G. Fawning; showing servile compliance

____ 8. TRIFLE   H. Introducing an idea subtlely

____ 9. FIE   I. Soon

____ 10. INSINUATING   J. Vulgar; humorously coarse

____ 11. GRATIFY   K. Criticism; disgrace; blame; shame

____ 12. MANDATE   L. Punishment; criticism

____ 13. OBSEQUIOUS   M. Something of little importance or value

____ 14. LINGER   N. Secretly plot

____ 15. CASTIGATION   O. Used to express distaste or disapproval

____ 16. ALACRITY   P. Promotion

____ 17. ANON   Q. Damages; marks

____ 18. BAWDY   R. Command; official instruction

____ 19. DELUDING   S. To be slow in leaving

____ 20. DISMAYED   T. Intelligence; humor

ANSWER SHEET - *Othello*
Multiple Choice Unit Tests

I. Matching	II. Multiple Choice	III. Quotes	IV. Vocabulary
1. ___	1. ___	1. ___	1. ___
2. ___	2. ___	2. ___	2. ___
3. ___	3. ___	3. ___	3. ___
4. ___	4. ___	4. ___	4. ___
5. ___	5. ___	5. ___	5. ___
6. ___	6. ___	6. ___	6. ___
7. ___	7. ___	7. ___	7. ___
8. ___	8. ___		8. ___
9. ___	9. ___		9. ___
10. ___	10. ___		10. ___
			11. ___
			12. ___
			13. ___
			14. ___
			15. ___
			16. ___
			17. ___
			18. ___
			19. ___
			20. ___

ANSWER KEY MULTIPLE CHOICE UNIT TESTS – *Othello*

Answers to Unit Test 1 are in the left column. Answers to Unit Test 2 are in the right column.

I. Matching	II. Multiple Choice	III. Quotes	IV. Vocabulary
1. F C	1. C D	1. C D	1. A Q
2. D I	2. C C	2. A B	2. Q T
3. B J	3. A A	3. C A	3. I K
4. J B	4. B B	4. D C	4. P N
5. H G	5. A B	5. A D	5. R D
6. I D	6. A C	6. B C	6. G A
7. C F	7. B A	7. C A	7. H P
8. A E	8. C C		8. S M
9. E H	9. C A		9. B O
10. G A	10. A B		10. K H
			11. M E
			12. D R
			13. C G
			14. F S
			15. J L
			16. O B
			17. L I
			18. T J
			19. N F
			20. E C

UNIT RESOURCE MATERIALS

BULLETIN BOARD IDEAS - *Othello*

1. Leave a portion of the bulletin board for the students' best writing assignments.

2. Write out some of the significant quotes from the play on colorful construction paper. Cut out letters to title the board SHAKESPEARE'S *Othello*.

3. Take one of the word search puzzles and draw it (enlarged) on the bulletin board. Write the clue words to find to one side. Invite students to take pens and find and circle the words in the time before and after class (or perhaps if they finish their work early).

4. If your library has a picture file, look through it to find people and scenes which look like they could represent characters or scenes from *Othello*. Post them on colorful paper on your bulletin board. If your library (school or public) does not have a picture file, try looking in some magazines for pictures.

5. Make a bulletin board by posting newspaper articles which show the ideas of revenge or jealousy.

6. Post articles of criticism about the play.

7. Make a bulletin board listing the vocabulary words for this unit. As you complete sections of the play and discuss the vocabulary for each section, write the definitions on the bulletin board. (If your board is one students face frequently, it will help them learn the words.)

8. Have one of your classes do a full production of *Othello*. Take pictures and use them for your future bulletin boards. (Your newspaper or yearbook staff would probably be glad to take the pictures for you!)

10. Do a bulletin board about careers in politics, government and/or the military.

EXTRA ACTIVITIES

One of the difficulties in teaching literature is that all students don't read at the same speed. One student who likes to read may take the book home and finish it in a day or two. Sometimes a few students finish the in-class assignments early. The problem, then, is finding suitable extra activities for students.

The best thing I've found is to keep a little library in the classroom. For this unit on *Othello,* you might check out from the school library other related books and articles about Elizabethan drama, history of the period, court life, etc. Also, you might include other works by Shakespeare (either in original text or simplified versions) and articles of criticism about *Othello*.

Other things you may keep on hand are puzzles. We have made some relating directly to *Othello* for you. Feel free to duplicate them.

Some students may like to draw. You might devise a contest or allow some extra-credit grade for students who draw characters or scenes from *Othello*. Note, too, that if the students do not want to keep their drawings you may pick up some extra bulletin board materials this way. If you have a contest and you supply the prize (a CD or something like that perhaps), you could, possibly, make the drawing itself a non-returnable entry fee.

The pages which follow contain games, puzzles and worksheets. The keys, when appropriate, immediately follow the puzzle or worksheet. There are two main groups of activities: one group for the unit; that is, generally relating to the *Othello* text, and another group of activities related strictly to the *Othello* vocabulary.

Directions for these games, puzzles and worksheets are self-explanatory. The object here is to provide you with extra materials you may use in any way you choose.

MORE ACTIVITIES - *Othello*

1. Have students design a playbill for *Othello*.

2. Have students design a bulletin board (ready to be put up; not just sketched) for *Othello*.

3. Use some of the related topics (noted earlier for an in-class library) as topics for research, reports or written papers, or as topics for guest speakers.

4. Find a film version of *Othello*, show it, and have students evaluate it in comparison to the play.

5. Have students act out the final act of the play on your school's stage. Assign parts. Other students should work together to design the actors' costumes and the set. Lines may or may not be memorized (teacher's decision). Perhaps you could present it to another section or two of English classes during your normal class period. (Provide a background narrative for the audience.)

6. Instead of making a whole production, assign a character to each student. Have that student design his or her own costume, memorize a short passage from the play, and recite the passage (in costume) in front of the class.

7. Have an Elizabethan day in your class. Have students dress up in Elizabethan costume, play music from the period, decorate your room as a castle banquet hall, and have students each bring something for a meal of the time. This will also require some research and planning on the part of the students.

8. Have students write one of the following letters:
    a. a letter from Roderigo to Desdemona
    b. a letter from Emilia to Desdemona, explaining the whereabouts of the handkerchief
    c. a letter from Iago to Cassio upon Cassio's promotion
    d. a letter from Cassio to Othello asking pardon and for his rank to be restored
    e. a suicide note from Othello
    f. a letter from Cassio to Iago a few weeks after the play
    g. a letter from Iago to Cassio a few weeks after the play

WORD SEARCH - *Othello*

All words in this list are associated with *Othello*. The words are placed backwards, forward, diagonally, up and down. The included words are listed below the word searches.

```
M T Q D Y H C H L Z D K T V F Q S J J P K X V Z
Q C T A J V D N T C M L Y A B V D Y F M N K W D
S G C W J P N I R A F Z K T N J G F Z N M O V D
O T H E L L O S E E M J E A L O U S Y E A R S Y
C X A I X O W R T H W J E W T A M D A Y L K B E
N P E B C G D N J R A I M G N S Y E G C D P W L
M S P K S A E O W Y M N F H N X Y O D E N B V W
I A G O S C S W V M U R D E R E Y R L S M A B P
H O L R O F O S G I B W T K R R V D C O E E I D
D O D N O P D N I D C A B A E C W E O V W D N B
T E N L H D W F F O H O E V M R N R R B K G O T
T I R E D C E Q G E W P A M V E C K H R O N V L
P P R H S W V R T Q S N V D I J H H O B A N V Z
V L R F R T S P I E K S F P P L J W I I S V Q D
L L A M C R Y X K G B Y E U T R I V T E V B N R
Y T B N E Q S A F J O T S D V K H A G M F A P M
Z W C T P I H S D N E I R F M N R B F G B G R S
F D T J C S B R A B A N T I O G F C J S V B T Q
X E F M Z R B R Q M Z H R V Q W Q S U R Z T C W
L R E P U T A T I O N M D X X S S H P L K Q K Z
```

ACT	GRATIANO	LODOVICO	SCENE
AM	HANDKERCHIEF	LOYALTY	SEEM
BIANCA	HATE	MOOR	SHAKESPEARE
BRABANTIO	HONESTY	MURDER	STABS
CASSIO	HUSBAND	NET	VIRTUE
CONFESSED	IAGO	NOBODY	WEB
DESDEMONA	INNOCENT	NOSE	WIFE
DIE	JEALOUSY	OTHELLO	WORK
DOG	JUDGEMENT	PLAN	YEARS
DREAM	KNAVERY	REPUTATION	
EMILIA	LETTERS	REVENGE	
FRIENDSHIP	LIES	RODERIGO	

CROSSWORD - *Othello*

CROSSWORD CLUES - *Othello*

ACROSS

1. The jealous Moor
4. 'There's magic in the --- of it.'
6. Iago plots to murder ----
10. Personal item belonging to Desdemona; Othello thinks she gave it to Cassio
13. Iago's wife; Desdemona's servant
15. Othello has to --- one person for a promotion; choose
16. These, found in Roderigo's pockets, were evidence against Iago
17. Othello's --- with Iago keeps him from questioning Iago's loyalty
21. Opposite of 'in'
22. 'Oh, damned Iago! Oh, inhuman ---!'
24. Droop
25. Partner to 'that'
26. Desdemona was killed in her bed----
27. Cassio's mistress
30. 'Men should be what they ---.'
31. Inside
32. Plot
36. Othello --- himself and dies
38. Emilia said Desdemona was ----
40. Othello's heritage
41. Value
42. '----, I myself. Farewell.'
44. Show gratitude
46. Singular past tense of 'to have'
47. Someone --- letters that ended up in Roderigo's pockets
49. Othello believes what he ----; looks at
50. Play division
51. Iago's motive
52. He is love-sick for Desdemona
53. Enemy

DOWN

2. 'So please your Grace, my Ancient, a man he is of -- and trust....'
3. Iago told lots of these
4. Emilia to Iago
5. Starts
7. Othello's wife
8. '----, ---, ---! Oh, I have lost my ----!'
9. 'Yet she must ---, else she'll betray more men.'
10. 'For naught did I in ---, but all in honor.'
11. Iago's actions ---- his guilt
12. A sudden breath due to shock
14. Iago lied & told Othello Cassio had a -- in which he cried out to Desdemona
16. Tells of the letters found in Roderigo's pockets
18. He was passed over for promotion
19. 'And out of her own goodness make the --- that shall enmesh them all.'
20. Othello to Desdemona
23. Brother of Brabantio
28. Coordinating conjunction
29. Becomes Lord Governor at the end of the play
30. Act division
33. Emilia's --- to Iago proves stronger than her --- to Desdemona
34. 'So I will turn her --- into pitch ....'
35. Motive for Othello's actions
37. Desdemona's father
39. '----'s plain face is never seen till used.'
42. 'The Moor ... will as tenderly be led by the --- As asses are.'
43. '... you shall more command with --- Than with your weapons.'
45. A ruler of a country
47. '--- on, My medicine, ---!'
48. Definite article
50. 'I -- not what I --.'

CROSSWORD ANSWER KEY - *Othello*

MATCHING QUIZ/WORKSHEET 1 - *Othello*

____ 1. VIRTUE   A. '----'s plain face is never seen till used.'

____ 2. REVENGE   B. Plot

____ 3. HUSBAND   C. 'There's magic in the --- of it.'

____ 4. PLAN   D. Becomes Lord Governor at the end of the play

____ 5. LOYALTY   E. Iago's motive

____ 6. INNOCENT   F. Personal item belonging to Desdemona; Othello thinks she gave it to Cassio

____ 7. HANDKERCHIEF   G. Emilia said Desdemona was ----

____ 8. CASSIO   H. 'I -- not what I --.'

____ 9. DREAM   I. 'So I will turn her --- into pitch ....'

____ 10. LODOVICO   J. Tells of the letters found in Roderigo's pockets

____ 11. SHAKESPEARE   K. Emilia's --- to Iago proves stronger than her --- to Desdemona

____ 12. NOBODY   L. Desdemona's father

____ 13. YEARS   M. These, found in Roderigo's pockets, were evidence against Iago

____ 14. BRABANTIO   N. 'And out of her own goodness make the --- that shall enmesh them all.'

____ 15. WEB   O. Author

____ 16. KNAVERY   P. Othello to Desdemona

____ 17. NET   Q. Iago lied & told Othello Cassio had a -- in which he cried out to Desdemona

____ 18. LETTERS   R. '----, I myself. Farewell.'

____ 19. AM   S. He was passed over for promotion

____ 20. IAGO   T. '... you shall more command with --- Than with your weapons.'

MATCHING QUIZ/WORKSHEET 2 - *Othello*

____ 1. SHAKESPEARE A. 'Men should be what they ---.'

____ 2. LOYALTY B. Iago's actions ---- his guilt

____ 3. CASSIO C. Becomes Lord Governor at the end of the play

____ 4. WIFE D. Tells of the letters found in Roderigo's pockets

____ 5. OTHELLO E. Iago's wife; Desdemona's servant

____ 6. REVENGE F. 'Oh, damned Iago! Oh, inhuman ---!'

____ 7. EMILIA G. Author

____ 8. FRIENDSHIP H. The jealous Moor

____ 9. SEEM I. Emilia's --- to Iago proves stronger than her --- to Desdemona

____ 10. GRATIANO J. Emilia to Iago

____ 11. WORK K. '----, ---, ---! Oh, I have lost my ----!'

____ 12. LODOVICO L. Iago's motive

____ 13. PLAN M. '--- on, My medicine, ---!'

____ 14. NOSE N. Emilia said Desdemona was ----

____ 15. REPUTATION O. Plot

____ 16. HONESTY P. Othello's --- with Iago keeps him from questioning Iago's loyalty

____ 17. CONFESSED Q. 'So please your Grace, my Ancient, a man he is of -- and trust....'

____ 18. INNOCENT R. 'The Moor ... will as tenderly be led by the --- As asses are.'

____ 19. DOG S. Brother of Brabantio

____ 20. STABS T. Othello --- himself and dies

KEY: MATCHING QUIZ/WORKSHEETS - *Othello*

Worksheet 1	Worksheet 2
1. I	1. G
2. E	2. I
3. P	3. C
4. B	4. J
5. K	5. H
6. G	6. L
7. F	7. E
8. D	8. P
9. Q	9. A
10. J	10. S
11. O	11. M
12. R	12. D
13. T	13. O
14. L	14. R
15. C	15. K
16. A	16. Q
17. N	17. B
18. M	18. N
19. H	19. F
20. S	20. T

JUGGLE LETTER REVIEW GAME CLUE SHEET - *Othello*

SCRAMBLED	WORD	CLUE
TIBRANOBA	BRABANTIO	Desdemona's father
NOTARGAI	GRATIANO	Brother of Brabantio
DOOLVOIC	LODOVICO	Tells of the letters found in Roderigo's pockets
HOTLOLE	OTHELLO	The jealous Moor
SOCISA	CASSIO	Becomes Lord Governor at the end of the play
GOIA	IAGO	He was passed over for promotion
GOREDIOR	RODERIGO	He is love-sick for Desdemona
DEEDNASOM	DESDEMONA	Othello's wife
AMILIE	EMILIA	Iago's wife; Desdemona's servant
CABANI	BIANCA	Cassio's mistress
KHFNAHRCEDIE	HANDKERCHIEF	Personal item belonging to Desdemona; Othello thinks she gave it to Cassio
RUDREM	MURDER	Iago plots to ---- Cassio
ERFPHIDSIN	FRIENDSHIP	Othello's --- with Iago keeps him from questioning Iago's loyalty
YATOLLY	LOYALTY	Emilia's --- to Iago proves stronger than her --- to Desdemona
TEETLRS	LETTERS	These, found in Roderigo's pockets, were evidence against Iago
MARED	DREAM	Iago lied & told Othello Cassio had a -- in which he cried out to Desdemona
SREAKAEHPES	SHAKESPEARE	Author
ELUSOJAY	JEALOUSY	Motive for Othello's actions
ROOM	MOOR	Othello's heritage
TAC	ACT	Play division
SILE	LIES	Iago told lots of these
CTOINNNE	INNOCENT	Emilia said Desdemona was ----
OFSEDCESN	CONFESSED	Iago's actions ---- his guilt
BUSNHAD	HUSBAND	Othello to Desdemona
FEWI	WIFE	Emilia to Iago
NEEEGVR	REVENGE	Iago's motive
CEENS	SCENE	Act division
LANP	PLAN	Plot
TASSB	STABS	Othello --- himself and dies
MA	AM	'I -- not what I --.'
SEARY	YEARS	'... you shall more command with --- Than with your weapons.'
SHOTNYE	HONESTY	'So please your Grace, my Ancient, a man he is of – and trust....'

SOEN	NOSE	'The Moor ... will as tenderly be led by the --- As asses are.'
MUDJEENTG	JUDGEMENT	'... yet that I put the Moor At least into a jealousy so strong that --- cannot cure.'
VERYNAK	KNAVERY	'----'s plain face is never seen till used.'
PANUTTORIE	REPUTATION	'----, ---, ---! Oh, I have lost my ----!'
RITVUE	VIRTUE	'So I will turn her --- into pitch ....'
TEN	NET	'And out of her own goodness make the --- that shall enmesh them all.'
EEMS	SEEM	'Men should be what they ---.'
BEW	WEB	'There's magic in the --- of it.'
ROWK	WORK	'--- on, My medicine, ---!'
OGD	DOG	'Oh, damned Iago! Oh, inhuman ---!'
EDI	DIE	'Yet she must ---, else she'll betray more men.'
DOOBNY	NOBODY	'----, I myself. Farewell.'
THEA	HATE	'For naught did I in ---, but all in honor.'

VOCABULARY RESOURCE MATERIALS

VOCABULARY WORD SEARCH - *Othello*

All words in this list are associated with *Othello* with an emphasis on the vocabulary words chosen for study in the text. The words are placed backwards, forward, diagonally, up and down. The included words are listed below.

```
A N O N B E G U I L E D B O M B A S T L F D X Q
T D D C V A P E S N E R J A E A R G A I E P Y W
P R V G A N W U X Y C J I S S A N S R T W T L Z
D E O O W S O D A P T O E P M E C D I A I C D B
J J R C C L T M Y S O E N J S I I E A R T E D X
M C J N U A S I E O C S Q T V N F F C T N I T R
H S L D I I T P G H B Y T I I R O A T R E P F Y
G N E L D C M I R A L S O U U N L C O W K B Q Y
K R R Y H E I S O S T U E S L A E B F V Z K X D
C R F K T C F O U N S I G Q Q A U N F Q H R Z F
J M S Y K H P O U Z Q N O K U S T T T T R C C R
Z P Y K F P I R S S I L D N E I N E N F C C G Z
F D M V M G E V O T H V C T Z E O E S Y R D H Q
N K P R E L M R A M B L I S M X M U T P E R M W
S S D R X R E U D K U S T R P I Q I S L M S G Z
F H G J L L N Z R I I L E Y D S U C U A F R C M
T E R S F I D N B U T F G E N Q P D L L A J C B
B Q F I S T R J Q R E I P A I B I I Q N X Q F F
N V R N F D Z E F R L M O N T N C Z G P Y T S J
Y T I N U T R O P M I L I N G E R E P R O A C H
```

ADVOCATION	DELUDING	INSINUATING	PROMULGATE
ALACRITY	DISMAYED	LASCIVIOUS	REPROACH
ANON	EGREGIOUSLY	LINGER	REQUISITES
BASE	EXPOSTULATE	MALICE	SATIETY
BAWDY	FIE	MANDATE	SHRIFT
BEGUILED	GRANGE	MARS	SUBORNED
BESEECH	GRATIFY	OBSEQUIOUS	SURFEITED
BOMBAST	IMPEDIMENT	PERDITION	TEMPEST
CASTIGATION	IMPORTUNITY	PERIL	TRIFLE
CONSPIRE	INCONTINENT	PERNICIOUS	WIT
CREDULOUS	INIQUITY	PREFERMENT	WOOED

VOCABULARY CROSSWORD - *Othello*

VOCABULARY CROSSWORD CLUES - *Othello*

ACROSS
2. Earnestly request
5. Vulgar; humorously coarse
9. Play division
11. Damages; marks
12. Confessional
16. Leave the stage
17. Something of little importance or value
19. 'Yet she must ---, else she'll betray more men.'
20. Introducing an idea subtlely
23. Conspicuously offensively
25. 'And out of her own goodness make the --- that shall enmesh them all.'
26. To be slow in leaving
27. Sin(s)
28. Becomes Lord Governor at the end of the play
30. Soon
32. Emilia to Iago
33. A cause; a path of action
36. 'Oh, damned Iago! Oh, inhuman ---!'
38. A king or queen ------s; holds power; rules
39. Act division
40. Othello's heritage
42. Heartbeat
43. Command; official instruction
44. Belonging to me
45. 'The Moor ... will as tenderly be led by the --- As asses are.'
46. The things Iago --- are as important as what he says; leaves out
47. 'There's magic in the --- of it.'
48. Having lost courage
49. Criticism; disgrace; blame; shame

DOWN
1. Puffed-up; pompous
2. Common; low in station
3. The condition of being over-filled or over-gratified
4. Punishment; criticism
6. Intelligence; humor
7. Diverted; taken away; also charmed or delighted
8. Farm; granary
10. Gullible
13. Used to express distaste or disapproval
14. Reward; indulge; satisfy
15. Iago told lots of these
18. Uncontrolled; unrestrained
21. Danger
22. Othello to Desdemona
24. Deceiving
26. Lecherous
29. He was passed over for promotion
30. Eagerness; quickness
31. Officially announce
34. Secretly plot
35. Violent storm
36. Iago lied & told Othello Cassio had one in which he cried out to Desdemona
37. 'I -- not what I --.'
39. 'Men should be what they ---.'
41. 'For naught did I in ---, but all in honor.'

VOCABULARY CROSSWORD ANSWER KEY - *Othello*

VOCABULARY WORKSHEET 1 - *Othello*

____ 1. Induced to commit a bad action or perjury
      A. Promulgate   B. Bawdy   C. Suborned   D. Linger

____ 2. Having lost courage
      A. Conspire   B. Surfeited   C. Dismayed   D. Linger

____ 3. Total ruin; damnation
      A. Perdition   B. Anon   C. Impediment   D. Mars

____ 4. Criticism; disgrace; blame; shame
      A. Peril   B. Preferment   C. Reproach   D. Satiety

____ 5. Soon
      A. Anon   B. Alacrity   C. Wit   D. Advocation

____ 6. Diverted; taken away; also charmed or delighted
      A. Preferment   B. Beguiled   C. Linger   D. Perdition

____ 7. Vulgar; humorously coarse
      A. Beguiled   B. Bawdy   C. Egregiously   D. Mars

____ 8. Secretly plot
      A. Surfeited   B. Insinuating   C. Deluding   D. Conspire

____ 9. spite; ill-will
      A. Fie   B. Deluding   C. Malice   D. Perdition

____ 10. Violent storm
      A. Reproach   B. Linger   C. Wit   D. Tempest

____ 11. Punishment; criticism
      A. Mandate   B. Linger   C. Deluding   D. Castigation

____ 12. Repeated requests
      A. Promulgate   B. Surfeited   C. Importunity   D. Pernicious

____ 13. Officially announce
      A. Deluding   B. Promulgate   C. Obsequious   D. Malice

____ 14. Eagerness; quickness
      A. Tempest   B. Pernicious   C. Alacrity   D. Anon

____ 15. Deceiving
      A. Deluding   B. Fie   C. Suborned   D. Peril

____ 16. Something in the way; a hindrance
      A. Requisites   B. Impediment   C. Castigation   D. Trifle

____ 17. To be slow in leaving
      A. Linger   B. Preferment   C. Incontinent   D. Requisites

____ 18. Danger
      A. Impediment   B. Conspire   C. Malice   D. Peril

____ 19. Farm; granary
      A. Beseech   B. Grange   C. Promulgate   D. Insinuating

____ 20. Fed to excess
      A. Surfeited   B. Dismayed   C. Perdition   D. Mars

VOCABULARY WORKSHEET 2 - *Othello*

____ 1. LASCIVIOUS A. Reward; indulge; satisfy

____ 2. IMPEDIMENT B. Deadly; destructive

____ 3. PERDITION C. Uncontrolled; unrestrained

____ 4. CONSPIRE D. Eagerness; quickness

____ 5. WIT E. Promotion

____ 6. PREFERMENT F. Command; official instruction

____ 7. PERNICIOUS G. Punishment; criticism

____ 8. INCONTINENT H. Repeated requests

____ 9. CASTIGATION I. Used to express distaste or disapproval

____ 10. GRATIFY J. Fawning; showing servile compliance

____ 11. ALACRITY K. A cause; a path of action

____ 12. IMPORTUNITY L. Confessional

____ 13. TRIFLE M. Something of little importance or value

____ 14. OBSEQUIOUS N. Lecherous

____ 15. ADVOCATION O. Something in the way; a hindrance

____ 16. MANDATE P. Danger

____ 17. FIE Q. Intelligence; humor

____ 18. SHRIFT R. Secretly plot

____ 19. PERIL S. Total ruin; damnation

____ 20. BAWDY T. Vulgar; humorously coarse

KEY: VOCABULARY WORKSHEETS - *Othello*

Worksheet 1	Worksheet 2
1. C	1. N
2. C	2. O
3. A	3. S
4. C	4. R
5. A	5. Q
6. B	6. E
7. B	7. B
8. D	8. C
9. C	9. G
10. D	10. A
11. D	11. D
12. C	12. H
13. B	13. M
14. C	14. J
15. A	15. K
16. B	16. F
17. A	17. E
18. D	18. L
19. B	19. P
20. A	20. T

OCABULARY JUGGLE LETTER REVIEW GAME CLUES - *Othello*

SCRAMBLED	WORD	CLUE
MATBBOS	BOMBAST	Puffed-up; pompous
EMERFNETRP	PREFERMENT	Promotion
QUIOOSESUB	OBSEQUIOUS	Fawning; showing servile compliance
GARNEG	GRANGE	Farm; granary
VICISALOSU	LASCIVIOUS	Lecherous
NEDGLDUI	DELUDING	Deceiving
ORTAGEMPUL	PROMULGATE	Officially announce
DILEEGUB	BEGUILED	Diverted; taken away; also charmed or delighted
CALTAYRI	ALACRITY	Eagerness; quickness
REEDUTIFS	SURFEITED	Fed to excess
STEMTPE	TEMPEST	Violent storm
SBAE	BASE	Common; low in station
YESTATI	SATIETY	The condition of being over-filled or over-gratified
QUETIRSSEI	REQUISITES	Requirements
MEMIDTIPEN	IMPEDIMENT	Something in the way; a hindrance
SEERGOLYIGU	EGREGIOUSLY	Conspicuously offensively
POTIRIDEN	PERDITION	Total ruin; damnation
THSFRI	SHRIFT	Confessional
CEHEBES	BESEECH	Earnestly request
DOOWE	WOOED	Courted; dated
POCRENIS	CONSPIRE	Secretly plot
UNTOPYRIMIT	IMPORTUNITY	Repeated requests
GASONATCIIT	CASTIGATION	Punishment; criticism
TOVADICNAO	ADVOCATION	A cause; a path of action
DORBENUS	SUBORNED	Induced to commit a bad action or perjury
ERODSLCUU	CREDULOUS	Gullible
RAPHEROC	REPROACH	Criticism; disgrace; blame; shame
ITW	WIT	Intelligence; humor
TUNIQYII	INIQUITY	Sin(s)
AEOXLTTSEPU	EXPOSTULATE	Reason earnestly
METNADA	MANDATE	Command; official instruction
DAWYB	BAWDY	Vulgar; humorously coarse
ITUGINNISNA	INSINUATING	Introducing an idea subtlely

ECNITONNIN	INCONTINENT	Uncontrolled; unrestrained
SAMR	MARS	Damages; marks
RELIP	PERIL	Danger
ANNO	ANON	Soon
IFE	FIE	Used to express distaste or disapproval
NERLIG	LINGER	To be slow in leaving
CENOPISIUR	PERNICIOUS	Deadly; destructive
FYRAGIT	GRATIFY	Reward; indulge; satisfy
LERTIF	TRIFLE	Something of little importance or value
MISDEYDA	DISMAYED	Having lost courage
CAMELI	MALICE	Spite; ill-will

www.ingramcontent.com/pod-product-compliance
Lightning Source LLC
Chambersburg PA
CBHW051414070526
44584CB00023B/3428